Celebrate
THE
Older
You

Celebrate THE OLDER You

BECOMING A WISER, WARMER, MATURE WOMAN

JO SCHLEHOFER

AVE MARIA PRESS   Notre Dame, Indiana 46556

International Standard Book Number: 0-87793-658-7

Cover and text design by Brian C. Conley

Printed and bound in the United States of America.

Library of Congress Cataloging-in-Publication Data

Schlehofer, Jo.
        Celebrate the older you / Jo Schlehofer.
                p.   cm.
        ISBN 0-87793-658-7
        1. Middle aged women—United States—Psychology. 2. Middle aged women—Religious life—United States.   3. Aged women—United States—Psychology. 4. Aged women—Religious life—United States.   5. Aging—Religious aspects—Christianity—Meditations.   I. Title.
HQ1059.5.U5S255   1998
305.244—dc21
                                                                98-3078
                                                                  CIP

With deep respect for all the women
I have worked with.
They have touched my life with insight and courage.
And with my love, appreciation, and heartfelt thanks to God,
my husband, children, grandchildren, and friends
who help me every day to celebrate my life.

Contents

Introduction

This book is written and dedicated to women over 50 who want to live their later years to the fullest, "to be all used up before I die," as Helen Hayes said of her life. Sooner or later, if we are lucky, we reach older maturity. This stage of life is a gift from God and offers challenges that women before us never had.

In struggling with my own post-menopausal years, as a marriage and family therapist, I have become empathetic with older women. Counseling led me to facilitate retreats and workshops to address the issues of post-menopausal women. The response has been overwhelming as women speak with me about their fears and concerns, their feelings and needs as they grow older.

The majority are concerned about health and their changing bodies. Judy, age 55, states, "I don't have the energy I used to have. I wake up each morning with a new ache. I'm concerned about osteoporosis. My cholesterol is high. I am fearful of taking estrogen because of side effects—I'm anxious, not knowing what to do." Nancy, 75, is concerned with aging itself. "My father, an Italian immigrant, always said, 'Old age is a disease in itself.'"

Like many of these women, we may be asking, "What is there to celebrate? How do I accept change in myself and in my relationships? Where do I go from here?" We must recognize that we need new directions, new goals!

Dottie, age 64, confesses, "Companionship in my marriage is lacking. My husband is coping in his own way with aging and retirement. We are growing farther and farther apart." In fact, most women are concerned about relationships in general. How do we parent our elderly parents and communicate with our adult children? How do we respond to our grandchildren without taking over from their parents?

Marilyn, age 61, wants to feel worthwhile and useful again. "I lost my job; my children are on their own. No one needs me."

Spiritual concerns are evident as we realize our mortality. Life becomes precious and fragile. We cry more. We empathize with strangers and animals and take on others' crises as our own. Our relationship with God seems inadequate. How do we make peace with God, our families, and ourselves? How do we get in touch with that deepest part of us, our souls?

This book addresses these challenges, not only to raise our awareness, which is a beginning, but to move us to work through these issues. It is only with understanding, effort, and support that we become women fully alive and able to celebrate life.

Because I find inspiration for my life in the psalms, I will try to pass on to you the opportunity to meditate and assimilate individually the meaning of the psalms appropriate for each of the sections of this book. There are also exercises sprinkled throughout. They are designed to give you more insight into yourself, to offer new directions, and to open up opportunities for growth.

The four major topics covered in this book were chosen from the concerns of the women I have encountered in my work. They have served as two-hour sessions in a "Celebrate the Older You" retreat or workshop that I present. I invite you to get away from the world and attend such a retreat. If you are unable to do so, this book can offer you the opportunity for inner renewal right where you are. With the love of the Father, the teachings of the Son, and the strength of the Holy Spirit we can turn the concerns of aging into a celebration of life.

It is my hope that this book will help you make the joyful song of Psalm 149 your own:

> *Sing to the Lord a new song,*
> *a hymn in the assembly of the faithful.*
> *Let Israel be glad in their maker*
> *the people of Zion rejoice in their king.*
> *Let them praise his name in festive dance,*
> *Make music with tambourine and lyre.*
> *For the Lord takes delight in his people,*
> *honors the poor with victory.*
> *Let the faithful rejoice in their glory,*
> *Cry out for joy at their banquet,*
> *With the praise of God in their mouths,*
> *and a two-edged sword in their hands. . . .*

—Psalm 149:1-6

Jo Schlehofer

Part I

"Mirror, Mirror on the Wall"

1
Snow White and the Seven Dwarfs

I was five years old in 1939 when I saw *Snow White and the Seven Dwarfs*, Disney's first full length animated film. To this day, I can still close my eyes and see the Queen—her tall figure, prominent widow's peak, high collar, and long swishing cape demanded my attention. I remember her famous question, "Mirror, mirror on the wall, who is the fairest one of all?" and the response of the eerie floating mask which set the whole story in motion. "Famed is thy beauty, Majesty. But behold, a lovely maid I see. Rags cannot hide her gentle grace. Alas, she is more fair than thee."

I naturally identified with Snow White. She was young, lovely, and did all the things I was going to do when I grew up. She loved animals, mothered the dwarfs, cooked, baked, and cleaned house. These were all the things I saw my mother do, and I modeled them in my play.

The dwarfs were adorable, funny, and protective of Snow White. What wonderful playmates they would make! At the toy store, I chose the Grumpy doll and my sister chose Dopey for our very own playmates.

The hunter's remorse spared Snow White's life. Her journey through the dark woods with knurled, twisted branches, owl's scary boos and floating logs turned alligators had me looking at shadows on my bedroom walls at night. I threw a temper tantrum and demanded that the light be kept on.

The Queen's transformation to a peddler-hag after drinking her magic potion was unforgettable. The voice, changed to a raspy cackle, her body shrinking and hunching into old age, bony fingers knotted and claw-like, the hooked nose with one protruding wart, two large circled eyes, and one tooth placed in that wicked grin assured me she was evil. The long, stringy hair topped with a black, pointed hat and black garb added the final touch. The close-up vision of the Queen's disguised face haunted my dreams for a long time.

My anxiety peaked as she convinced Snow White to bite into the poison apple. I thought she had died when she fell to the ground. She was as still as my pet rabbit was when he died. I sat on the edge of my chair willing the dwarfs to arrive in time. What a disappointment when they didn't! I cheered as the dwarfs chased the witch up the mountain in the violent storm and a bolt of lightening struck her and she fell into oblivion.

When the prince kissed Snow White on the lips and she awakened from a deep sleep, I was mesmerized. Best of all was the dream of myself on that beautiful white horse, riding off to the prince's castle to live happily ever after.

It wasn't until the Walt Disney Company released the film on video that I viewed the movie again. As I watched the film with my grandchildren, I had the same emotions I had when I went back to the neighborhood where I grew up. My past romantic expectations dissolved and became realistic. Everything looked smaller, less scary, and disappointing.

Snow White seemed only a child, no more than a fourteen-year-old. Her innocence and naiveté did not seem to fit in our present world. She was vulnerable.

I saw the Queen symbolically rather than realistically. She embodied the greed and selfishness that haunts us all. I recognized her as a type that was portrayed in many other animated movies that followed this first one.

I was surprised at the minor part the Prince had. He appeared briefly, but played the important role of the rescuer. When all seemed hopeless, he was there to make it all better. He's the figure we all hope for.

Each dwarf was familiar to me, no longer as wonderful playmates but now as aspects of myself. Their personalities were parts of me, journeying through life. The exaggeration of the dominant traits made each personality easy to spot.

Doc was the leader. Stressed by his "job," his stuttering gave him away. It's tough to be in a role where others depend on you.

Grumpy played the role of devil's advocate. He was a skeptic. He created a hard shell as a defense mechanism to protect his fragile, inner self. As he allowed Snow White to penetrate his shell, he became vulnerable.

Dopey had the carefree attitude we would like to have. He slipped through life as the bar of soap slipped through their hands while they were washing for dinner. His attitude provided humor for those around him. But because Dopey would do whatever the dwarfs wanted him to do, he became their pawn.

Happy didn't like confrontations. He "reframed" an unpleasant incident with a rosy glow. He hid his frustration by trying to make light of happenings. Decisions must have been difficult for him because he hadn't learned that the only person you can change is yourself.

Sleepy escaped life by sleeping. He didn't have to make decisions because he was tired. Perhaps his underlying feeling was depression, causing him to postpone decisions that had to be made.

Sneezy had allergies. He was aware "there was dirty work afoot." His resistance was low. By not feeling well, he could escape responsibilities. Sneezing could also have been a way to get attention. The dwarfs certainly rallied around him, trying to stop his sneezes.

Bashful was labeled by the dwarfs, and he lived up to his name. He represented passivity. He would never intrude on others. Although he wasn't aware of it, because he wouldn't respond assertively to fulfill his needs, he intruded on himself.

While I can relate in some way with each of the dwarfs, the one dwarf whom I see as most like me probably would be Happy. Like him, I try to avoid confrontation by wanting to fix people. In my family of origin, I played the rescuer. I remember when my sister was two years old and began to talk; she stuttered. I took on the job of protector even though I was only four. I didn't give her a chance to talk because I talked for her.

My tendencies to fix things also held true in my relationship with my parents. I followed all the rules and tried to please them. When my parents would argue in their stormy Italian way, I would try to intervene and make it better. By the time I was a teenager, I became the mediator for peace.

As mature women, we need to develop a self-image that does not fall into the Snow White syndrome of helplessness and dependency. Snow White's helplessness left her vulnerable to the greed and selfishness of the Queen. She became dependent on the dwarfs for her physical care and on the prince to rescue her from the Queen's wrath. Her happiness was defined through the Prince. A confident self-image allows us to identify and fulfill our own need and wants as long as we are physically and emotionally able.

Part I of this book is called "Mirror, Mirror on the Wall. . . ." In this part we will be reflecting on our self-image. Some of the questions we'll be seeking answers to are: What is self-image? Why is it important? How is it formed? What challenges does our self-image confront as we age? We will also look into childhood messages and expectations that have formed our self-image. By looking at what goes into forming our self-image and studying those parts, we'll learn how to adjust our self-image appropriately as we age.

FOR REFLECTION

- How old were you when you first saw the movie *Snow White*?
- Do you remember the feelings you experienced as a child?

❦ Rent the video, make some popcorn, and watch it again. Think about the feelings you experience as you observe the characters. How do these feelings differ from the feelings you experienced as a child? Which feelings are the same?

❦ Which dwarf do you see as most like you?

❦ Describe the characteristics of the dwarf you have chosen as you see him. How are they similar to yours? How are they different?

PSALM REFLECTION

O God, within your temple
we ponder your steadfast love. . . .
Go about Zion—walk all around it,
note the number of its towers.
Consider the ramparts,
examine its citadels,
That you may tell future generations;
"Yes, so mighty is God,
our God who leads us always!"

—Psalm 48:9, 12-13

In Psalm 48, we ponder God's temple, his being, his love. The psalm asks us to "go about Zion," the unconquerable city of Jerusalem. As we walk around it, we notice the number of its towers which provide strength, the ramparts which provide security, so that all may know God's power.

Let us see ourselves as Zion. Our soul dwells in the holy temple of our body. Walk around inside mentally. Notice your strengths and weaknesses. Are there some towers and ramparts that need to be strengthened to form a healthier self-esteem in the image and likeness of God? What are some of the defenses have you used for security? Do they still serve a purpose or are they not needed at this time in your life?

2
You in the Mirror

Sixty-two-year-old Frances came to me for counseling with symptoms of anxiety and depression. She was heavier than was healthy, unkempt, and placid. Frances felt her religious beliefs were threatened. She was brought up in a strict Catholic environment during the time when the church was unforgiving. Her image of God was strict, powerful, and not loving. She followed all the church rules in detail and did her best to please God. Then God deceived her. He took her only daughter away at five years of age.

Frances felt rage and didn't know where to direct this strong feeling. She feared God's wrath and damnation to hell, so she turned this rage onto herself. She became depressed, eating and sleeping too much, isolating herself from family and friends.

As we worked together in counseling, Frances became aware that as a young girl with a strict, unbending father and passive mother, she hadn't known what to do with her feelings. She blamed herself for not being "good enough" and kept trying harder to please her parents. Her self-image was poor because if no one loved her, not even God, she was worthless.

I helped Frances visualize how the picture she had of herself from the past affected her thoughts and feelings in the present. She needed to accept her feelings and to learn to express them in healthy ways. Throughout her life, her feelings and actions were not congruent; they didn't match. Anxiety developed subtly and then became full-blown. She had not grieved properly for an unforgiving father, an unsupportive mother, and the death of her child. Her only recourse was the defense mechanism of depression.

Because Frances was able to question her experience, she was able to develop a healthy self-image. We too may need to engage in a similar process of asking ourselves questions like these:

What is a healthy self-image?

Why is it important?

What kind of challenges affect our self-image as we age?

How did we get where we are?

How do we make it better?

On our journey to becoming physically and psychologically healthy, each of us has needs which must be met. Physical needs are more obvious: proper food, healthy sleep patterns, exercise, and effective medical care. But psychologically we need to feel safe, loved, worthwhile, esteemed, and motivated. We also need to nurture the spiritual part of ourselves, that part that transcends the physical life and continues into eternity.

Self-image is how we see and feel about ourselves. Self-image determines how successful we are in fulfilling our needs and becoming psychologically healthy. It has three facets: how we see ourselves, how we would like to see ourselves, and how we perceive others as seeing us. The more congruent these facets are, the more we sparkle and shine. A healthy self-image would include:

an ability to take an interest in more than self and one's material possessions,

an ability to relate present experiences to past experiences,

an ability to form warm long-lasting relationships,

a possession of realistic skills, abilities and perceptions to cope with challenges of life,

a compassionate regard for all living things, and

a unifying philosophy of life which transcends human meaning.

For Reflection

Answering the following questions will help you learn more about yourself.

- ❦ What is my basic personality (which dwarf am I)?
- ❦ Do I basically enjoy being myself or would I rather be someone else?
- ❦ What do I do especially well?
- ❦ Do I think I am important enough to have time for myself?
- ❦ How do I make time for myself?
- ❦ How do I feel when I receive compliments? Can I say a simple "thank you," or do I downplay my assets?
- ❦ Do I need people around me all the time? Can I be alone without being lonely?
- ❦ Do I accept projects to be recognized or because they need to be done and I enjoy them?
- ❦ Do I make impossible demands on myself?
- ❦ Have I formulated goals for my life? What are they at this present state of my life?

Self-image can be changed. It is continually evolving. By the age of five, our self-image has deep roots in us. Throughout our journey in life, we continue to be exposed to circumstances that mold us. How we react to these circumstances based on our self-image determines the comfort and fit of the mold. The earlier we are molded in positive ways, the easier it is to feel esteemed.

As we age, placing ourselves in a healthy environment allows us to continue to develop ourselves to the fullest. Each of us needs to determine what is a healthy environment for us and then pursue it. Our environment should not impose constructs and conflicting values that would hinder our self fulfillment.

Emily grew up in a family that covertly taught that success was measured in materialistic possessions. They lived in a beautiful home in an affluent neighborhood, drove expensive cars, and had fashionable clothes. She learned at an early age that it was important to impress others. When she married and had a family of her own, she and her husband did not earn enough income to live as she was accustomed to living. Emily struggled to keep up appearances, but because she could not live up to the image she had of herself, her self-esteem deteriorated. She directed her frustration and anger toward her husband in subtle ways, undermining their relationship. Emily did not know how to value herself in any other way but materialistically.

Developing self-esteem consists first of understanding how important a positive self-image is. The way we see ourselves will determine how we feel about ourselves and how we live our lives, set goals, and actualize them. Self-esteem is the ingredient that determines the friends and companions we choose, the kind of long-lasting relationships we form, and the way we parent and develop careers and interests. It determines how we feel about aging and how we accept the responsibility to search for a meaningful life in our later years.

Early childhood experiences, significant others, parenting, and society have played roles in the development of our self-esteem. We also cannot discount how our genetic predispositions interact with our surrounding environment to affect our self-image.

Recognizing our true feelings and taking responsibility for them will prevent us from trying to be "all things to all people." If we have received more positive approval than negative criticism in our life's confrontations, then less incongruity between who we are and who we want to be will exist. We do not have to negate our feelings to get the approval we need.

Because Frances did not have her parents' unconditional love, the kind of love we need to feel esteemed, she had to ignore her feelings and tailor her actions to please them. This pattern followed her in all her relationships, including her relationship with God. She transferred the image of her father to God as children do. God became her father. He looked like him, acted like him, and loved her conditionally as her father did. Her "child voice" was persistent. "If you behave this way, then I will love you."

Giving ourselves permission to accept and feel feelings is a "stepping-stone" to liking "me." All feelings are part of our human nature. What we are held accountable for is our expression of those feelings in sociably acceptable ways: we may not physically or emotionally hurt ourselves or others, or destroy property.

Self approval is necessary to feel important and worthwhile. We think well of ourselves when we are affirmed unconditionally. In this type of environment we feel esteemed. The values we have formed from experiencing life need to match our self-concept. Initially, we need constant approval from others, but if we grow and mature in confidence, we are able to depend on our own selves for approval. If these two are at odds, distortion will occur. This state of distortion may manifest itself as tension, anxiety, maladjustment, defensiveness, and finally helplessness or depression. This affects how we relate to others.

AGE CHALLENGES SELF-IMAGE

Challenges to self-image as we age can upset the balance of congruency between our actual self-concept and our ideal self-concept. We live in a youth-oriented society. Even though the baby-boomers are reaching middle age, marketing is slow to change. Most cosmetic and hair commercials use models of twenty-something and younger. We cannot compete with those young beautiful bodies. No wonder we look at our aging bodies with disdain!

Aging is full of surprises. Each morning we awaken to something that wasn't there before. A hair has popped out where it doesn't belong. Gray hairs curl among strands of dark brown hair. We get out of bed rolling to the side, slowly feeling a new ache or pain. As we look in the mirror we are certain we must be looking at someone else. It takes longer to get ourselves ready to meet the day; stronger toothpaste, more lotion for parts of our bodies we never paid attention to before, and of course, the morning urgency to get to the bathroom before all else.

Daily we see wrinkles increase. Because society labels wrinkles as undesirable as warts, we look for remedies from anti-wrinkle creams to plastic surgery. Instead of wrinkles representing wisdom and maturity, we are bombarded with the illusion that we do not have to age. We need to accept aging as a growth process and the beginning of change into a new life. We age from the day we are born. Like a fine wine, it takes years to develop the best flavor of life.

Another challenge is the fear of dependency. Our aging bodies may make us more dependent on others than we want to be. It is painful to think of losing our independence. It is important that we take inventory of ways we are in control of our lives. We feel helpless without control. Do I like myself enough that if I am lonely I can reframe my loneliness to just being alone? If my weight is unhealthy, can I control what I eat and how I exercise? Can I be assertive in communicating my wants and needs by being aware of my feelings and expressing them in nonthreatening ways to those around me? Being assertive is difficult if we confuse humility with passiveness.

Humility is strength and purpose as Christ demonstrated, not the passivity which allows others to make decisions about living for us.

Our aging bodies are also incongruous with our feelings. We are little girls in aging bodies. Our minds want to run, dance, flirt, and make angels in the snow, but our bodies restrict us. Sometimes we feel that if it wasn't for our bodies, we could live forever. But we do live forever. There will be a time when our bodies will no longer hamper us and we will soar freely. Helen Hayes stated so eloquently, "When I die, I want to be all used up." To be used up means to live each day to the fullest, to squeeze all we can out of our physical being and to concentrate on developing our spiritual side, that dimension that lives forever.

I remember when I was ten years old, I loved to read Nancy Drew mysteries. I was so eager to read them, that I risked punishment by reading under the covers with a flashlight when I was supposed to be sleeping. How can we recapture that zest as we age? Finding or experiencing something new according to our capability and doing it, is a start. In Part III, we will be discussing how to develop an individual mental health portfolio to keep intellectually vital.

Finally, we grieve more as we age. There are more occasions to experience illness and the death of family members and friends. Mortality becomes a reality, and we grieve for our losses. When we lose a job, go through a divorce, experience a changing nest, or lose a part of our body, we grieve.

Frances transferred her feelings and her "unfinished grief" with her family of origin to God. Transference happens when we redirect our feelings onto others who are not the primary source of the original interaction. As we live longer, we seem to experience more counter-transference issues, issues from our past that have not been worked through and that are transferred to others in our present life.

Judy explained, "My best friend died of breast cancer. I am saddened and have a feeling of emptiness in my life. There is a nagging, anxious feeling that permeates me. How could she have endured her illness and its treatment of chemotherapy and radiation to no avail? Could I bear the pain if it happened to me? How much more time do I have?" Judy became more aware of her mortality with the death of her friend. She needed to work through the "unfinished business" of what death meant to her.

In working through grief, it helps to reframe it. Think of grief as change. We grieve or change as we meet crises. In fact, without crises we probably would not grow to a new level. In counseling, I sometimes create a crisis to promote growth. It is change we need to cope with. We need to progress through the stages of grief to heal and enable ourselves to go on with our lives.

Frances worked to progress through the stages of grief in counseling. She had denied that it was her parents that prevented her from accepting her feelings and being able to express them, not God. She stopped blaming herself for not being perfect enough and stopped bargaining with God. Frances became aware of her angry feelings that led to depression and anxiety and began to understand depression as a "time-out" to sort through it all. Finally she began to accept, "This has happened; it is over. I must get on with my life."

Most of the time, we are able to work through these challenges. Sometimes we need help and support to prevent us from becoming stuck in a stage without the "know how" to move on. Knowing when we are stuck and need help requires insight and self-esteem. This is part of the challenge of moving from dependency to independence.

Let us praise the God who is always with us in the words of Psalm 48:

Yes so mighty is God,
our God who leads us always!

3
Through Ages and Stages

All of us carry mirror images of ourselves that we received from parents, teachers, and peers as we developed our self-image in ages and stages. If most of the reflections were approving and supportive, we developed a positive self-image. But if they were not, they interfered with the process of building our self-esteem. In this chapter we'll become more aware of these past reflections, so that we can recompute and change those that blocked the healthy development of our self-image.

The earliest mirroring came to us during infancy and preschool days. Margaret Mahler, an ego psychologist, observed children in natural settings for five years. She noted examples of how children separate and individualize from a parent during the first three years of life. Her research determined that it was critical for the primary caregiver to have emotional availability while this psychological process was occurring. Her research explains the development of self-image.

Let us follow this process of separation, individualization, and self-image development in our lives. From birth to one month of age, we were in an autistic stage, dominated by the physical needs of hunger, sleep, and comfort. Up to four or five months of age, we perceived our primary need as being an object, mother. But we saw her as part of ourselves. This stage was highlighted by our first real smiles. We were beginning to invest in another person. Mom's sensations were ours. If she was anxious, so were we. If she was calm, we reflected calmness. We "mirrored" or imitated what we saw.

After five months of age, we began to differentiate our self from mother. We became more aware of the external world. We began to scoot and move away from her. Were we fixated in this stage of psychological development due to poor parenting, we would have had difficulty distinguishing our self from others in later years. Our self-image would depend solely on how others see us.

From eight months to fifteen months, we continued to move away from our "significant other" by crawling and walking, always checking back, wanting mom close by for support and security. The beginnings of "this is me, that is you" was emerging. In this stage, we first dealt with good and bad experiences. If our mother was loving, gentle, supportive, and redirective in her parenting, we experienced ourselves as all good, mirroring her behavior. But if she slapped our hands every time we reached out, giving no redirection, we saw ourselves as bad. We thought only good or bad. We did not have the ability to integrate the two. It is during this stage that personality disorders can begin. Frustration and anxiety at this stage can lead to the "all black and white" personality, with no ability to see shades of gray.

From fifteen to twenty-four months, we continued to explore the environment around us. We were curious and cautious—wanting to explore, but not sure of what was there. We began to have a realistic view of mother, realizing she also had needs. Now we were involved in a three-dimensional view of mother, loving her, hating her, and seeing characteristics in her that were different from ours. We developed empathy. If she cried, we wanted to make it better. Now we could hold a mental representation of mom; we had what psychologists call an "object constancy." It was during these months that we overcame the splitting of good and bad. We could integrate bad and good and not lose mother's love. She was there for us! This recognition of support and constancy was important in how we visualized ourselves. Our self-esteem was developing.

By thirty-six months, we fully internalized mother. We could stay with someone else without crying because we could keep a mental picture of her with us at all times. She would come back. We were individualizing. Our self-image was being esteemed.

The second stage of self-imaging development moved to mirroring other members of our origin and extended family. We developed physically, intellectually, emotionally, socially, and spiritually. We became "old enough to . . ." by listening and watching others. The more special someone was to us, the more we mirrored them. At three, it was important for us to please. We did lots of imaginary play trying to find out who we were. We were trying to distinguish between fact and fantasy.

During school years this process of mirroring continued. There was growth from dependency to independence. Feelings came into full force. Frustrations mounted. Anger was foremost as we tried to adjust to peer relationships, rules, and teacher restrictions. Our conduct probably was inconsistent as we tried to please so many in order to keep or gain affection. As we grew into the middle grades, we watched our peers' behavior. Their approval of us became more important than the adults around us. What they thought of us determined how we felt about ourselves. Self-image was in transition as mirroring moved from parents, to extended family, to teachers, and to peers.

The next phase of self-image development occurred in us as young adults, while we were learning skills for a life-long career. It was during this period of life that we were seeking long-lasting relationships, including a life partner. Still wanting and needing acceptance and unconditional love, we may have made selections to please others rather than making choices based on self-esteem.

As we matured, we developed a realistic view of self that enabled us to mix feelings and actions in a way that did not lower our self-esteem. Developing this view involved tasks of being able to move toward:

> *Emotional maturity*: accepting our feelings and emotions and expressing them in constructive ways;
>
> *Social maturity*: having feelings of secure acceptance by peers and the ability to develop long-lasting relationships;
>
> *Emancipation*: moving toward self-control and reliance on self for security;
>
> *Intellectual maturity*: a demand for evidence before acceptance, a desire for explanation of facts, stable interests, and a reconciliation of interests and abilities;
>
> *Use of leisure time*: implementing hobbies and interests;
>
> *Philosophy of life:* interest in understanding principles, behavior guided by moral principles based on conscience and duty, and a belief in faith;
>
> *Identification of self:* a moderately accurate perception of self, a good idea of others' perception of self, and integration with the ideal self, that is, self-esteem.

These tasks are, "going about Zion (ourselves), walking around and in it, noting the number of its towers—considering the ramparts and examining its citadels." This is the task still before us, knowing who we are and how we feel about ourselves as we live in the present and on into eternity.

4
Voices from Childhood

As we lived through our childhood, we were given messages from those around us. The more meaningful the person in our lives, the more important and long lasting the message. These childhood messages from significant others became voices in our ego that shaped our self-image.

Some of the messages erased our fragile reasoning, interfering with our logical reality. By confronting these inner voices from our past, we gain the ability to determine which messages we need to let go of and which will help us to further develop our self-esteem.

Our inner voices determine our self-talk, spurring us into action. With every situation that we meet in life, there is "self-talk" before we act. That inner talk has been developed from our life experiences with others. Rather then following these messages blindly, we need to stop and listen to our inner words. This process will help our decision-making process override those voices from the past which keep us from attaining self-esteem.

"I'LL LOVE YOU IF. . . ."

One strong childhood message that many of us experienced is that love is conditional. This was love given based on behavior rather than on our self. The following story illustrates this:

Peggy has painful arthritis. She came to see me because she was depressed and ready to give up. She was tired of the pain and the inability to do all the active things she used to be able to do. It was a chore for her even to bathe or shower. But she had made sure that she had no emotional support from her family or friends. It was a sign of weakness if she talked about herself. That would be complaining.

When Peggy was a young child, she remembered falling off her new tricycle and breaking her arm. She screamed with pain. Instead of receiving the comfort she needed, her mother's response was, "Now that isn't so bad. Stop crying. It doesn't hurt that much. You shouldn't have been riding your bike on the edge of the sidewalk anyway."

Even at an early age, Peggy realized the unspoken rule in her family. Do not express feelings. That would be a sign of weakness. Peggy wanted to please her mother, so she bore the pain that followed the break in silence. Her self-esteem was weakened as she blamed herself for causing the accident and not living up to her mother's expectations.

Mother was passing on the process of giving conditional love that she had learned from her family of origin, love that was based on behavior. Behavior needs to be separated from love. Behavior is learning to adjust to social rules and is taught. Unconditional love is all encompassing, given freely with no strings attached. The love that God gives us is not attached to behavior. It is freely given. It is unconditional, steadfast love. "Oh God, within your temple we ponder your steadfast love. . . ."

Because we need unconditional love to be fully human, we continually strive to please others to get the love we need. We spend our lives trying to please others, many times at the expense of our self-esteem. We allow others to intrude on us and accept this behavior by responding passively. Because we have not accepted that we cannot please everyone all of the time, our self-image is reduced.

When I was in second grade, I idolized my teacher. I wanted her acceptance and love and would do anything to please her. In art class one spring day, we were making hyacinth flowers on a card for Mother's Day. There was a sample put up on the board for us to follow exactly. We cut out little purple squares to paste on our card to resemble each individual part of the flower. I loved to make things. Being in a seven-year-old stage of perfection, I thought I had created a masterpiece. When I was done, I raised my hand proudly. When the teacher came over to my desk, she looked at my work, proceeded to hold it up to the class and stated, "This is not how you are to do this. It doesn't look like my picture." She proceeded to pull off my little flowers that I had worked so diligently at and redid my card. I was devastated. Not only did I not please her, but I blamed myself for not being smart enough to make a picture exactly like hers.

For a long time, my attempts at creativity became mechanical. My coping strategy was to stay away from any art classes and not do any art work. The day of reckoning came in college when I had to take an art class to graduate with my teaching degree. Fortunately, my professors were excellent teachers, and encouraged and praised my work. Since that time in college, I have taught art in my elementary school classes and have done watercolor paintings. But most importantly, I learned to do my best and please myself.

"You will do it my way. . . ."

The childhood message of control also enters our ego and plays havoc in our relationships. We all need to feel in control of our lives. As we age, we become more aware of this because more uncontrollable situations seem to arise. We need to be able to determine which situations we can control and which we cannot. If we have learned from our childhood to use control as a coping strategy, we may have difficulty letting go under any circumstances.

When Ann was two years old, she remembers sitting in her high chair and not wanting to eat her oatmeal. She cried and screamed "No, no" as a two-year-old would do. Her father sternly stated, "You will eat this oatmeal or have nothing else to eat all day." At lunch time, the cold oatmeal was placed before her. She looked at mother and cried for something else. Mother said nothing. At dinner the same cold oatmeal was put before her. She was so hungry, she choked on the paste as she ate it. Father stated, "You will never say no to me again." She never did. Ann felt completely out of control. She felt abandoned. No one was there to protect her. She left home at 18 and vowed no one would ever control her again.

Ann came to counseling with relationship problems. She had been married three times and couldn't sustain long-lasting relationships. She was too controlling and couldn't determine what was healthy control and what was not. Her aggressive behavior intruded on other people's rights.

"I CAN'T DO THIS. . . ."

Many of us have experienced episodes of obsessive (thoughts) compulsive (actions) behavior. Tendencies such as perfectionism, procrastination, and addiction need to be dealt with. When we use these behaviors as coping strategies, our "ramparts" become weakened. When others are indifferent, we reflect these tendencies as we try harder to please, to get the unconditional love and approval we need.

Perfectionists are not driven by ambition but by fear of rejection. Perfectionism interferes with the ability to grasp the "big picture" of life. We become occupied with details, rules, lists, and schedules. Because perfectionists picture themselves as not good enough and they revert to trying to please others to gain acceptance, their self-image is low. Procrastination is one way of coping with low self-image. Decision-making is either avoided or postponed because of fear of making a mistake.

Adeline felt that her parents were trying to live their lives through her. She was an only child born to older parents. Adults were her role models. She was pushed into piano lessons at an early age. Her parents hovered over her practice sessions and insisted she learn a new piece each day. They monitored all her homework from school and expected perfection. Adeline dreaded bringing home report cards. She became fearful and anxious. Physically, she bit her nails and began to stutter. As an adult she wouldn't begin projects that she thought she would fail. She didn't want to try and found herself procrastinating. This behavior became so severe that she wouldn't even do projects that had to be done.

Addiction is usually labeled as obsessive compulsive behavior but differs from true obsessions or compulsions because pleasure is primary. This behavior can have long-range effects on those exposed to it. Children raised by an addictive parent can, as adults, develop addiction or co-dependency as coping strategies. The atmosphere in such a family is unstable. Whether the addiction is alcohol, drugs, rage, or relationship-oriented, there is inconsistent behavior. Family members are caught in double binds, situations in which there is no winning. You are "damned if you do, or damned if you don't."

Jane's father was an alcoholic. The rule that was spoken in the family was to be loving and affectionate. But when Jane approached her father to give him a hug, she was pushed away. Later she was labeled as a cold child because she never showed affection. Being caught in a double bind creates insecurity and anxiety. Jane learned to form a hard shell around her to protect her against others. She carried this shell to age 50 when her father died. Her grief surfaced unfinished business and brought her into counseling to work on her self-esteem.

These different uncomfortable childhood messages that we have examined seem to be woven together by the single thread of a poor self-image. The coping strategies which these messages created were necessary for survival during childhood, but now in adulthood need to be let go of. They are destructive in our relationships with ourselves, with others, and with God. Continuing to love yourself conditionally, pleasing others at the expense of yourself, striving for perfection because of fear of rejection, and giving in to addictive behavior are coping strategies that prevent us from developing a "steadfast love" in our relationships.

PSALM REFLECTION

What we had heard we now see
in the city of the Lord of hosts,
In the city of our God,
founded to last forever.

—Psalm 48:9

You have heard about how self-image is formed. The stages of development have been explored. Uncomfortable childhood messages have been uncovered. Now picture yourself as the city of the Lord, "founded to last forever."

FOR REFLECTION

Use these questions to look prayerfully into yourself.

- Are you overly concerned about your appearance?
- When a birthday comes around, are you frantic?
- Do you feel that everyone else is perfect? Do you experience feelings of jealousy and envy often?
- Do you avoid tasks that need to be done because you are fearful that they will not be done perfectly?
- Do you work so slowly that creativity is lost?
- Do you have a low tolerance for mistakes? Even if you do well, do you only notice what could have been better?
- Are you fearful of trying something new?
- Do you always try to please others even at the expense of your feelings?

❦ What childhood messages are you struggling with at this time in your life?

❦ How are they affecting the way you feel about yourself?

Let us continue to "build a city of God."

5
Little Girls in Aging Bodies

We are all little girls in aging bodies. No matter how old we are, we are still that little girl that skipped rope, roller skated on the sidewalk, skinned knees, wore braids with barrettes or ribbons, and ate ice-cream bars from the ice-cream man on the bicycle.

When I was a little girl about nine years old, street games were popular. We lived on a quiet street in a suburb of Chicago shaded by large elm and maple trees. It was a fitting setting for a game I especially liked to play because I was good at it. I could win. It was called, "Mother, May I?"

My playmates and I lined up on the curb. I was comfortable teaching the game and giving directions. Even at an early age, I did so eagerly. The others would follow. Usually we chose Alice Mae to be "Mother" as she was heavier and couldn't run as fast. She was always willing.

Our goal was to get across the street without being tagged. We had to follow orders from "Mother" and take the appropriate number of giant steps, baby steps, or scissor steps. If we forgot to say, "Mother, May I?" we had to go back to the curb and begin again.

While "Mother" wasn't looking, we could try to make a run for the other side and be home free. When free, we could try to "save" others trying to come across by tagging them without "Mother" catching us. If we were tagged by "Mother," we became her helpers and had to help her capture others, and so the game continued. I was a fast runner; I saved my playmates many times.

It wasn't until later in my life in my work as a psychotherapist, that I could reflect how like my nine-year-old self I became as an adult. The delight I took in saving my friends during "Mother, May I?" played a part in my becoming an educator and a therapist. It satisfied my teaching and rescuing needs. But because my life experiences allowed me to be congruent with my little girl self, I could feel comfortable with myself as an adult.

Perhaps another reason the game caught my fancy was its focus on the role of "Mother." "Mother" represents the inner voice we all struggle with in forming our reality. As we develop through the various stages of growth toward maturity, we subconsciously ask permission from our "parent within" each step along the way. What happens when we ask our inner parent's permission to take a "giant step" and get a no in response? We feel we cannot take the step because we have mirrored a low self-image reflected to us by our caregivers.

Sally, an only child, tells her story: "Whenever I wanted to try something new, my parents held me back. They wanted me to stay their little angel. I was always too young—too young to ride a bike, too young to go to the corner store, too young to date—no wonder it is difficult for me to take a giant step."

Do we ask permission to take only baby steps because we have grown up being cautious? Life is dangerous. We must move slowly and cautiously. Rita remembers being afraid to play in the yard alone. "Mom was afraid I'd fall off the swing or fall and skin my knees. I can't remember ever being outside alone. I'm still anxious when I am alone."

Do we dare to be creative and take a different kind of step, the "scissor step," or do we run to the other side and feel guilty? As a child Beth was told never to play with Miranda. She was black; she was questionable. When her friend became ill, she went to visit her anyway. To this day she still struggles with guilt for not obeying her mother.

Parent voices can erase our natural child and form a reality ego that is not truly who we are. It is important to tangle with these internal voices to live more completely and congruently with who we are. Only then will we nurture our self-esteem and inner peace. Unwilling compliance with these inner voices creates a false self. We can, however, get rid of our false self. But to do so we need to:

> observe the connections we have with others,
>
> become aware of how we feel,
>
> express these feelings in open and honest ways,
>
> and reach chosen goals with "Mother's" full awareness.

FOR REFLECTION

Settle in a comfortable chair and relax. Think back to your childhood to when you felt most like yourself. Think of an incident that made you feel cozy and comfortable.

- ❦ What were you doing?
- ❦ What person or persons were nearby?
- ❦ Did you feel supported?
- ❦ What was the outcome?
- ❦ Would you be able to repeat that incident as an adult? Why or why not?

Karen Horney, a well-known psychoanalyst, stated, "Female personality comes to be lodged in an idealized feminine image rather than in the authentic identity a female possesses as a child." We are most like ourselves between the ages of eight and ten, usually uninhibited, independent, and adventurous.

This is the time between fantasy and reality that creates a positive self-image. At this age goals are seldom criticized, choices are made and usually supported. There are lots of opportunities for thinking, planning, and putting goals into action.

Somewhere along the line, however, this little girl gets lost. Conformity has taken hold, society dictates, rules abide, and hiding skills are developed as she matures to womanhood. We need to get in touch with that little girl to become who we really are. We need an anchor for awareness.

A GUIDED MEDITATION

Relax in a comfortable chair. Take three deep breaths counting slowly to five as you breath in and again count to five as you breath out. As you slowly feel yourself softening, picture yourself as an eight- or nine-year-old.

You are walking up to the front door of your house where you lived at the time.

What does it look like? Do you remember the color of your house?

Is there a porch? Are there stairs that lead to the front door?

Open the front door and enter your house. What do you see? Are all the rooms on one floor, or are there stairs leading to the bedrooms? Take your time and walk through the living room, kitchen, and where you used to eat. Can you remember colors, textures, and objects?

Move on to your bedroom or the place where you slept. What furniture, pictures, curtains, and toys are in the room? Look at the special things that are yours. Look over everything slowly. Pick up an object that is very special to you. Was it a book, a doll, a toy, or an article of clothing? Why was it so special to you? Take your time to examine your object. When you are ready, take your object with you and say good-bye to your room. Walk slowly back to the front door. Say good-bye to your house and walk out the front door.

Slowly bring your image of your object to the here and now. How does it feel to you now that you are an adult? Use the image of your object as an anchor image to keep you in touch with the real you.

Exercise

I have encountered this picture at many workshops and have used it myself with groups. Although I don't know who the artist is, I have always been grateful for his or her work. I invite you to study it and then to respond to the reflection questions.

🐛 Which little girl is most like you?

🐛 How does she typify your self-image?

🐛 Which little girl represents the self-image you would like to have?

🐛 Is it the same?

🐛 Which one do you think others would perceive to be you?

6
What Do You Expect?

Expectations play an important role in the development of our self-image. Expectations involve our decision-making process, and because we often act according to them, they shape our self-image.

For example, if I have an expectation that my energy level will be as it was when I was in my twenties, I'll keep a fast pace. I may wonder why I am so exhausted by nightfall. While my mind wants to go, my body says no. I become discouraged when I do not accomplish all I want to do in one day. My self-esteem weakens; I feel there is something wrong with me.

Expectations are caught from childhood messages. When expectations are met, when we live up to our goals, we feel good about ourselves. When they are unmet, or when others' expectations are not congruent with our goals, we feel less competent. Met expectations indicate realistic goal setting. But when expectations are too high, feelings of frustration and helplessness can set in. Alternatively, when our expectations are too low, we are not challenged enough. Then boredom and depression may result.

We have expectations about all areas of living. Some common expectations are:

Relationships that are loyal, devoted, loving, and exclusive;

Positive support from "significant others";

Enough support to prevent loneliness;

A smooth, comfortable transition into old age;

The ability to accept change and move on in life;

Knowing how to nurture a positive self-image;

Feeling secure and safe;

Feeling useful by being able to contribute to society;

Maintaining independence though old age;

Realizing financial security.

You may have several others. Add them to this list and create a picture of your expectations. This list will help you see what it is you want from aging.

How do we change our expectations to keep from lowering our self-image? First we need to understand how we formed these expectations. What childhood messages were in play? Nancy's parents were immigrants from Czechoslovakia. They worked hard to survive poverty. There was no leisure time. Nancy formulated the expectation that idleness was not tolerated. She had difficulty making time for herself. That would be wasting time. She had labeled leisure time as laziness.

Developing realistic step-by-step goals helps us meet our expectations. If your goal is to live wellness, it must be divided into sub-goals like steps on a ladder to enable you to reach the top by climbing up one step at a time. Your first step might be eating healthfully; step two, planning an exercise program tailored to your needs. Developing a new interest would bring you to the third step. The top step would be to nourish the spiritual part of you. Each of these sub-goals might need smaller steps so your expectation of living wellness can be met.

Exercise

On a piece of paper, draw a line down the middle of the page. On the left side of the paper, list your vision of the ideal older woman. Here are some suggestions that may help you: What does she look like? How does she react to situations? What are her interests? How does she relate to others? What is her spiritual make-up?

Now on the right side, follow the same pattern and list how you see yourself. How many discrepancies are there? If there are too many, your expectations may be too high; they may also be to low. The more your expectations of the ideal older woman match your image of yourself, the better you will feel about yourself.

Stand in front of your "magic" mirror. Ask yourself, "What things do I like about myself? What are the things that I would like to change? Are these things that can be changed? If so, how can I start right now? If I change these things, will I be the "fairest of all"?

7
Developing Self-Esteem

We have explored what a healthy self-image is, why it is important, and what challenges affect the way we see ourselves as we age. We learned how we got to where we are. Now we will look at how we can make it better.

As we noted in Chapter four, all of us engage in "self-talk" before we act. When a situation occurs, we dialogue with our inner voices and then react. Our self-talk is often so much a part of us that we are unaware of it happening.

Diana has a hearing problem. She purchased a hearing aid and found that it was not helping her. Her friend told her that she paid too much for it, she had been taken advantage of. As the days went by, Diana's self-talk told her that it was too late to do anything about it. It would be too much of a hassle to try to remedy the situation. Her action was not to do anything about it. She would have to live with the problem.

Diana acted passively. As a result, she weakened her self-image by not getting what she wanted. If her self-talk had been more logical, she would have taken a more assertive stance, and the results would have esteemed her self-image and not demeaned it. The more logical the self-talk, the more assertive the responses will be, and the more esteemed we will feel.

As we respond to challenging situations, our behavior can be aggressive, passive, passive-aggressive, or assertive.

Mary's family took her out to dinner. She ordered meat-loaf because she had dental work done and her teeth still ached from the trauma. She liked her meat cooked well-done and mentioned this to the waitress. When it arrived, it was red inside and not what she wanted. How would each of these four stances have shaped her response?

Aggressive: Mary pouted and called loudly for the waitress to come over to her table. She spoke loudly and rudely as she scolded the waitress for not bringing what she wanted. Mary was aggressive. She intruded on the waitress's rights, embarrassing her in front of others.

Passive: Mary looked at the meat, decided it wasn't what she wanted, but didn't want to cause a scene. So she ate her dinner without looking up or saying anything. Mary demeaned herself; she didn't feel good enough about herself to get what she had ordered.

Passive-Aggressive: Mary put her fork into the meat and saw it was rare. She cringed and complained to her family what a terrible restaurant this was. She complained to those who didn't cook or serve the meal. Instead of taking care of the problem, she avoided the confrontation by putting the responsibility on her family.

Assertive: Mary quietly called the waitress over. She explained that she ordered the meat well-done and would appreciate this being taken care of. The waitress did not feel intruded upon or put on the defense, her family did not have to listen to the complaints, and Mary got what she wanted.

The first three behaviors exhibit low self-image; she intrudes on others or demeans herself. When her self-talk is more logical, she responds assertively, esteeming herself and others.

Exercise

Become aware of your self-talk. Pick a situation in which you were not happy with your response.

❦ What was the inner dialogue that prompted this response?

❦ What reaction would you prefer to have made?

❦ What would your self-talk have had to be?

Self-talk can be changed. Once you are aware of your self-talk and where it is coming from, you can substitute a more logical talk that will create responses to situations that will not trigger guilt, anger, or other uncomfortable feelings.

AFFIRM YOURSELF

Creating and absorbing affirmations helps us to develop self-esteem. Affirmations are powerful tools for programming the mind. By inputting positive statements, we push out the negative thoughts that lower our self-esteem. In affirming ourselves, we counteract our negative self-talk.

We can create affirmations for different areas of living. The following basic affirmation may be all that is needed to jump start self-esteem: "I am a lovable, worthwhile, and unique person created by God. There is no one else in the world like me." Affirmations need to be repeated often. In the morning upon awakening and before going to sleep at night are especially effective times to engage in self-affirmation. They may be offered as a thanksgiving prayer to God.

Throughout the day, you can pause and say your affirmations. It is important not to have too many to say at one time. Three or four work well. After you feel they have become part of you, you can originate two or three more. Writing them down and placing them in view, on the bathroom mirror, on the refrigerator door, or on your calendar will help you to remember to say them faithfully. Some examples might be:

I will take full responsibility for my health.

I will take charge of the direction my life goes.

I will not say "should not have." I will let go of the past.

I will accept change and grow from it.

I do not have to prove myself to others, only to myself.

Formulate three or four affirmations that fit you. Write them down on a small card or post-it note and place them where you will see them each day. Say them often, until they become your self-talk. Developing logical self-talk and incorporating affirmations into our internal "citadels" will build strong "ramparts." The more secure we feel, the easier it will be to let go of the childhood messages that interfere with our self-esteem.

Other steps you can take to feel lovable and worthwhile are:

> *Give yourself permission* to express feelings that have been locked up inside. Don't hesitate to ask others to hold, touch, or hug you.

> *Care for your body* in the best possible way. It has to last a lifetime.

> *Get help* with jobs that are difficult to do alone.

> *Praise your accomplishments* and take others' compliments deep into yourself.

> *Find ways* to do what you want to do and have what you want.

> *Avoid* people who make you feel unloved or worthless.

Change happens all around us. Remember when "on line" meant hanging clothes on the line outside to dry, prime time was spending time with our families not watching television, and gay was a feeling we expressed, not a sexual orientation? As we live longer, it becomes more difficult to adjust to change. Change tampers with our self-image by diminishing our self-esteem. We fight change as we struggle to keep comfortable. We experience feelings of helplessness as we are swept away in the sea of change.

For every change we encounter, we grieve for our loss. We usually deny that change is happening. When we wake up one morning and experience hip pain, we ignore it hoping it will go away. As the pain progresses and goes on for several weeks, we begin to think that something may be wrong. We feel anger as we cannot do the simple things we were used to doing, standing on our feet for several hours or going for our regular walk without pain. Other feelings are triggered. Guilt: "I shouldn't have worked so long in the yard pulling weeds." Depression: "Will this pain ever go away?" Fear: "Something may be terribly wrong. What if I have bone cancer?" Then we begin the bargaining process. Surely a novena of prayers will make the pain go away. We promise not to eat chocolate for a month. Finally we go to the doctor and accept the diagnosis of osteoarthritis. We begin to develop a new lifestyle.

Change is scary because it throws us into the unknown. We don't know where we are headed. We are like a ship riding a storm at sea, trying to find land. Our goal is to accept the change and loss, to adapt to the changing environment by letting go of what was, and to move on in life. We may not be able to control the change, but we are in control of how we will deal with it.

Knowing and affirming ourselves and feeling loved and worthwhile make our ship sturdy and secure. Developing a mental health portfolio that we will discuss later in this book will help us set goals to move on in our life, to direct our ship. Being aware of stress as we weather the storm of change is important. What yellow warning light does your body give you? Do you pay attention to that backache, headache, stomach pain, high blood pressure, dizziness, or neck strain? Feeling tired, anxious, or irritable more than occasionally can be a sign of stress. Loss of appetite, sleeplessness, or grinding teeth while sleeping can also be signs of stress. The emotional part of us is woven through the physical part. When one dimension is stressed, so is the other.

To deal with the stress of change, we need coping skills. These skills are the capable crew we have chosen to steer our ship: learning to be assertive enough to ask for what we need and want, becoming aware of our expectations, and setting realistic goals are skills that we can learn. They can become an accurate compass for us.

A healthy attitude makes steering the ship over rough waters easier. When we feel good about who we are and what we are doing, it is easier to be positive, to be optimistic about the future. Humor is the fuel that our ship needs to keep on going. Reaching out to others who are going through the change with us also helps us accept the change and land on safe ground. We are now ready to try a new adventure, meet someone new, adopt a new pet, try a new hobby, or change our scenery or routine. We have been able to "let go" of the old and accept the new.

Talking to ourselves develops a healthy attitude toward making mistakes. We can reframe what has happened by admitting the mistake. "I really blew that one. OK, it happened. What did I learn to prevent this from happening again?" Or, "I did a great job. How did I ever think of that?"

Use stress busters to relax, to give your body a chance to heal. A warm lingering bath, listening to your favorite music, a walk in nature, or reading a book are ways to take you away from the stress. Writing your feelings in a journal will help you keep track of the effect stress is having on you.

Exercise

Try this relaxing exercise to unwind when you feel uptight.

Sit in your most comfortable chair. Close your eyes. Wiggle yourself into the chair until all your body parts feel comfortable. Take a deep breath. Hold it for five seconds. Then slowly let out the air to the count of five. Do this three times.

With your eyes still closed, imagine you are going down in an elevator. Down, down you are going, deeper and deeper into yourself. Keep breathing. When your elevator reaches the bottom floor, press the open-door button. Step out of the elevator. As you look ahead you see a warm, sunny light at the end of the hall. Walk toward the inviting light. Feel its warmth as the light surrounds your body. Let go of any tension and let the warmth relax your body. Stay as long as you like and savor the warmth.

When you are ready, walk back to the elevator. Press the up button and feel yourself slowing rising as you take deep breaths. When you reach the top and the doors open, open your eyes slowly and return to your world, feeling more relaxed and energized.

There are many relaxing exercises you can do. It doesn't matter which one. What is important is that you do it, that you find the time for yourself to help you cope with change.

One favorite spiritual meditation I do often to get me through my storms of change may help you also. I keep this famous quote on my desk. I find new insight each time I read it.

> *God grant me the Serenity to accept the things I*
> *cannot change,*
> *the Courage to change the things I can,*
> *and the Wisdom to know the difference.*

Feeling good about ourselves is a basic need for achieving a sense of total well-being and inner peace. Our goals, expectations, and achievements are based on this premise. All of us experience misfortunes, loss, and emotional and physical pain at one time or another during our life. It is not the incidents themselves, but how we react to them that affects our well-being and self-esteem. Be kind to yourself.

Psalm Reflection

Read Psalm 48, "The Splendor of the Invincible City" once more.

> *O God, within your temple*
> *we ponder your steadfast love. . . .*
> *Go about Zion—walk all around it,*
> *note the number of its towers.*

Consider the ramparts,
examine its citadels,
That you may tell future generations;
"Yes, so mighty is God.
our God who leads us always!"

—Psalm 48:9, 12-13

Compare Zion to "your house," yourself.

❦ Are you a city of God that is a joy to yourself, to God, and to others?

❦ Have you explored all your rooms, all the parts that make you whole?

❦ What strengths and weaknesses do you see?

❦ How do they affect your self-image; what does your magic mirror say?

❦ Have you allowed God to enter each room? In what way?

❦ How has this improved your self-image?

❦ Are you able to "let go" of childhood messages that stop you from feeling good about yourself?

Reflect on other ways this psalm can be a mirror of your self-esteem.

Part II

You and Me

8
Connecting with Self, Others, and God

Webster defines relationships as "connections." Connecting includes three basic kinds of relationships: intrapersonal, friendship with self; interpersonal, friendship with others; and suprapersonal, friendship with God.

Jesus summarized the whole of the Old Testament in the Two Great Commandments: "You shall love the Lord your God with all your heart, with all your soul, with all your mind, and with all your strength. . . . You shall love your neighbor as yourself" (Mk 12:30-31, NAB). From our perspective, we can also see in them the three basic types of relationships with self, with others, and with God.

The underlying foundation of friendship begins with the friendship we have with ourselves. In the process of developing self-esteem, we are developing skills to interact with others. How we feel about ourselves determines how fulfilling our interpersonal and suprapersonal relationships will be. A healthy intrapersonal relationship is vital to forming the seeds of long-lasting and meaningful relationships with others that can sprout and grow.

In order for relationships to grow, there needs to be a commitment to connecting. This entails honest communication, awareness of feelings, and a willingness to express these feelings in words and behavior in ways that do not harm the relationship.

Madeline couldn't remember when it was exactly that her mother abandoned her emotionally. She thought it began after her father died and Madeline and her family had moved away. Her mother would seldom call, and when she did, she said hurtful things. She would attack Madeline's husband, her parenting skills, and what she was doing in general. Madeline reacted passively to the assaults. She buried her hurt feelings and tried harder to please her mother. All to no avail; the rejection continued.

This went on for years. It wasn't until Madeline was in her sixties that she realized she had to express her feelings to her mother. Her mother also needed to take responsibility for their relationship. But sadly, the outcome was not favorable. Her mother responded by not communicating at all. The relationship withered and died.

A one-sided relationship cannot exist. Counseling helped Madeline to accept her loss and move on to more meaningful relationships. Commitment is needed by both parties in a relationship if the friendship is to endure. This can be true even in marriage counseling. If one or the other is not committed to the marriage, counseling will not be successful. But when a two-sided commitment is there, trust is the by-product. It is the fertile soil in which the roots of relationships receive their nourishment. A trustful relationship is void of the games we have learned to play to manipulate outcomes that favor us.

Psalm 15, which will be our biblical touchstone for this part, offers a number of characteristics of a trustful relationship:

> *Who does not slander a neighbor,*
> *does no harm to another,*
> *never defames a friend;*

Whoever acts like this
shall never be shaken.

—Psalm 15:3, 5

Babs and her mother were caught up in the game of, "You don't spend enough time with me." Mom felt Babs did not give her enough attention. When Babs would come to visit her on the weekend, Mom would detail all her aches and pains and complain about how lonely she was. Babs would try to defend herself by again stating this was the only time she could visit her. Guilt would consume her and she would end up sacrificing her family and job by spending more time with her mother. Mother received what she wanted: more attention from Babs; and Babs received what she needed: relief from her guilt.

Such games fulfill our needs in covert but damaging ways. Relationships are weakened when communication is manipulative. Sometimes we are so caught up in a game that we do not even realize we are playing one.

FOR REFLECTION

Think about the games you have played that may not be congruent with the real you.

- Do you play the game of innocence so as not to take responsibility for a relationship?
- Do you use your relationship for power and control?
- Do you smother the other person with affection and monopolize their time for fear of losing them?
- Do you agree with others to avoid confrontations?
- Do you feel you are OK, but others are beneath you?
- Are you condescending?

Games prevent relationships from being honest and long-lasting. Exploring the games we play brings awareness of how we relate to others. How do we know if we are playing a game? When we play a game, we mask our true feelings, and there are hidden messages in our actions. Look for hidden messages like: "Nobody loves me," "How dare you!" "Yes, but. . . ," or "I deserve to do what I want to do." When we're sending these messages indirectly, we're probably playing a game.

Helen's story is a case in point: Helen is having difficulty communicating with her husband since he has retired. Everything he does seems to annoy her. He is always underfoot. She resents not having the time she used to have for herself. When he wants to do something with her, even though she might enjoy the activity, she refuses. If he wins his point, she gives him the silent treatment. The underlying message is, "I deserve to do what I want to do."

Manipulative actions are usually learned during childhood and continued if they get results. A parent may push a child to defend herself in a confrontation with a classmate by saying, "Are you going to let her get away with that?" The child may learn to fulfill her needs aggressively, manipulating others into friendship forcefully. Unfortunately, relationships based on fear are not long lasting.

FOR REFLECTION

Think about an interaction when you were manipulative.

❦ What was the game you played?
❦ What do you think the hidden message was?
❦ Where do you think this game originated?
❦ What effect did the game have on the relationship?
❦ If you are still using this manipulation, how can you stop the game?
❦ What communication skills might help you move on?

Knowledge is the water that makes relationships grow. The more we understand ourselves and those we care for, the more we can love them. The more we look inward and learn about ourselves, the more honest, open, and loving we can become to others. Learning about those we love and care for develops a long-lasting relationship. Learning more about God creates an environment for the prayerful development of a richer spiritual life.

Unconditional love is like sunshine to a relationship. By loving unconditionally, we do not try to change others but allow them to be who they are. We do not put restrictions on the relationship: "I'll love you when . . . " or "I love you, but. . . . " Feelings play an important role in helping us to love unconditionally. Sympathy helps us to share and understand others' feelings and interests. Empathy, the capacity to participate in others' feelings, not only makes us aware of their distress but gives us the desire to relieve that distress. Compassion is a feeling that allows us to walk in others' shoes, to see things as they do. It helps us to love unconditionally.

Monica is waiting in line at the bank. She is in a hurry as she is late for a dental appointment. There are several people ahead of her in line. The line is moving very slowly. The longer she waits, the more irritated she becomes. The person behind her bumps into her. She turns around, ready to angrily reprimand him, when she sees he is using a cane. Her angry feelings melt away, replaced with compassion. She offers help to him.

FOR REFLECTION

Think of a relationship in which you love unconditionally, and then one in which your love is conditional.

- ❧ What is the difference in your feelings towards each?
- ❧ How do you feel when you are loved unconditionally?
- ❧ Who has loved you unconditionally?
- ❧ Give an example of someone who loves you conditionally. How do you feel about this relationship?

PSALM REFLECTION

Reflect on the description of unconditional love in the following psalm.

> *Bless the Lord, my soul;*
> *do not forget all the gifts of God,*
> *Who pardons all your sins,*
> *heals all your ills,*
> *Delivers your life from the pit,*
> *surrounds you with love and compassion,*
> *Fills your days with good things. . . .*
>
> —Psalm 103:2-5

9
Exploring Our Relationships

Now that we have taken a first look at the three kinds of relationships that are integral to our growth, let's explore them further.

MAKING FRIENDS WITH YOURSELF

The friendship we make with ourselves will determine the friendships we build with others. This friendship with self rests on our ability to love ourselves unconditionally for who we are, not what we do. When we can admit our mistakes, learn from them, and move on to self-forgiveness, we grow in a process that will enhance our friendships with others. Like all relationships, intrapersonal relationships involve our self-concept.

Loving unconditionally incorporates kindness, forgiveness, and honesty. What does it mean to be kind to yourself? Making time for yourself by doing enjoyable activities expresses kindness. Pampering helps us to feel special. Give yourself permission to eat a banana split occasionally. Buy silk underwear or a new fragrance. Get a new hairdo, a pedicure, or a massage to be sure you are making time for yourself.

Forgiving ourselves can sometimes be difficult, but humor goes a long way in helping us forgive our mistakes. "I can't believe I threw my red T-shirt in with a whole load of white clothes. What was I thinking? Oh well, I will look like the Pink Panther for a while. It sure won't happen again."

Humor springs from inside us. Events may trigger laughter, but we need to be open and living in the present to accept the trigger. When we laugh, the world looks bright. We are more open to feeling loved and giving love unconditionally.

An active parishioner greeted Father after Mass. As they were talking, Father noticed a newcomer he had recently met. "Carole, I'd like you to meet Mary. She's a teacher in the religious ed. program. You two will have a lot in common, both being teachers." After Father left, both women looked confused. "Is your name really Carole?" asked Lois. "No, it's Judith." "Well, my name is Lois. Father cannot remember names," replied Lois. They both laughed as they shook hands. A spirit of forgiveness enabled them to see the humor in the situation.

Honesty with self often calls us to pay attention to our feelings. Be honest about your feelings: give yourself permission to experience them without guilt, and to express them honestly. When we express our feelings with "I" statements, we do not intrude on others. "You" statements are often interpreted as blaming others. At the same time, they keep us from fully owning our own emotions.

Be a friend to yourself. Set reachable goals that will help you feel useful and fulfilled and move you on in life. Having a new interest or completing a new hobby or project creates a feeling of accomplishment, contentment, and well-being. We feel worthwhile and esteemed.

JoAnn retired as a medical attorney. She hesitated to give up her work, but her husband insisted as he was retired and wanted time to play together. At first it was wonderful having time to do fun things. But after a while, JoAnn missed her work and the feeling of accomplishment it provided. A friend suggested she do volunteer legal work for seniors. She volunteered her time one day a week at the senior center. As she helped seniors understand their medical benefits, her client load increased. She was able to work out a balance of work and play that was agreeable to her husband. She enjoyed helping others and felt good about herself in the process.

Interpersonal relationships also depend on our self-concept. If our self-concept is strong, we will mirror others who share our lives in healthy ways. We'll be able to be for them without losing ourselves. But if it is weak, our tendency will be to become what others want in a relationship and to lose ourselves.

We all feel most comfortable with people who are similar to us. But as we age, it becomes more difficult to expend the effort to make new friends. We become more critical of what is different. We feel uncomfortable and tend to protect our boundaries. When this happens, the range of our friendships becomes narrow and limited. Developing friendships interpersonally fulfills a basic human need. We were not created to be alone. As the scripture says, "It is not good for the man to be alone. I will make a suitable partner for him" (Genesis 2:18).

Learning to Relate to Others

Our first attempt at interpersonal relationships was in our family of origin. As an infant, the first time we recognized and smiled at familiar faces, we were developing friendships.

My mother related to me the story of how I tried to make friends with my newborn little sister. My sister was sleeping in her bassinet in the dining room. I had a lollipop and was walking toward the bassinet. I stood up on my tip toes and leaned over the edge. I could see the baby was awake. My lollipop tasted so good, I wanted to share it with her. Being only two years old, my coordination was shaky. As I reached over to give her a taste, I made contact with her eye. She screamed and Mom came running, scolding me for what I had done. I'm sure I cried, not understanding why my mother was upset, as I only wanted to share my treasure with my sister.

We begin socializing through play. The first stage of social development is individual. We played alone with Mom close by. Between two and three years of age, we played alongside other children and began some interaction. Our attempts were not always successful and sometimes ended in tears or tantrums. We were in the stage of parallel play. After three, we progressed to group play and were able to interact with other children in imaginary play. Playing house, modeled after our home life, was always a favorite.

On one occasion, in one of my parent education classes, the parents of two pre-schoolers and I observed them playing house. The little girl was busy making dinner and soon ordered the little boy to sit down and eat. He obligingly did so and exclaimed with gusto, "Don't tell me you are serving me this crap again."

In the elementary grades, we socialized with others in team play. In the primary grades, we were concerned about fairness and tattling was endless. Any second grade teacher knows the familiar, "Bobby pulled my hair!" "Suzie spilled my milk!" or "Tommy hit me." As pre-teenagers, we wanted a few close friends of the same sex to share secrets. Hiding places, forts, or club houses were critical for secret meetings. As teens, we became consumed with locating a "significant other." How many times did I perform my theatrical death if my idol did not call?

During this social development, we began the process of emancipation, moving away from our family of origin and using our communication skills to fulfill our needs and wants. If communication was manipulative, we may have had problems in our relationships. But if we communicated in positive ways, we developed long-lasting, healthy relationships.

As we grow in our adult relationships, we go through stages. When we first meet people, we begin at the "How do you do?" or acquaintance stage. We know very little about them. It is difficult to know if they are being genuine or masking their true selves. We listen and take our cues from their body language. If we like what we see, then we begin the process of bonding.

I'd like to share some of the skills I have learned as a therapist to assess clients during the first session. My first goal is always to bond with the clients and to gain their confidence for future sessions. I pay attention to body language, nervous nuances, eye contact, and congruency of words and actions.

When we meet someone socially for the first time, we can pay attention to these dynamics and proceed with a process of assessing and bonding that is comfortable for us.

FOR REFLECTION

❦ When you meet someone for the first time, how do you assess the person?

❦ What characteristics do you look for in an acquaintance that attracts you to them?

❦ How do you begin the process of bonding?

❦ Think of an example of a person you have recently met. Do you want to nurture a friendship? Why or why not?

When you decide you want to pursue a relationship, you enter a second level of growth, becoming friends. Usually you will bond with someone easily if your personalities, values, and interests are similar. Friendships develop over time. They are comfortable and predictable relationships. Even when you are separated for a long time, you are able to pick up where you left off at your last visit.

Not long ago, I undertook a special project. With the help of my alumni association, I located and invited several of my college friends to my home for a reunion. My feelings were bittersweet. I hadn't seen these women in forty-one years. I was excited at the thought of being reunited, but fearful of how the years might have changed us. I had attended a small Catholic women's college that became like my family. I treasured the memory of those relationships. What if those memories were shattered? I needn't have worried. We spent four glorious days together and picked up right where we left off forty-some years ago. New memories were created, and promises were made never to let time get away from us again.

The third stage of interpersonal relationships is the deepest. It is intimacy. There is a body and soul connection with significant others. The cement in intimate relationships is trust. When you give yourself completely to a person, you have entered the deepest friendship we are humanly capable of. We take the risk of becoming vulnerable.

As Jesus walked among others on earth, he modeled what true friendship is about. His relationships with his disciples, both men and women, his care for the poor, and his ability to confront in a healthy way provide us with a strong model. He lived the description of a truly whole person in Psalm 15:

> *Lord, who may abide in your tent?*
> *Who may dwell on your holy mountain?*
> *Whoever works without blame,*
> *doing what is right,*
> *speaking truth from the heart;*
> *Who does not slander a neighbor,*
> *does no harm to another,*
> *never defames a friend;*
> *Who disdains the wicked,*
> *but honors those who fear the Lord;*
> *Who keeps an oath despite the cost,*
> *lends no money at interest,*
> *accepts no bribe against the innocent.*
> *Whoever acts like this*
> *shall never be shaken.*
>
> —Psalm 15

When Jesus died on the cross for us, he gave us the most intimate relationship that could be experienced. There is no deeper love one can give to another than laying down one's life.

> *I give you a new commandment; love one another.*
> *As I have loved you, so you also should love one another.*
> *This is how all will know that you are my disciples,*
> *if you have love for one another.*
>
> —John 13:34-36

OUR CONNECTION WITH GOD

In addition to the *intra*personal and *inter*personal relationships we share, there is the *supra*personal relationship we have with God. This spiritual friendship is a mysterious and wonderful relationship that touches the deepest part of us, our soul. We marvel at God's love for us and ask ourselves, "Lord, who may abide in your tent? Who may dwell on your holy mountain?" We desire to abide with the Lord and nurture our spiritual dimension, to develop our connection with God. God communicates and touches us through divine love in our souls. He also communicates with us through nature, people, and unexplained happenings. God is always active, but we need to keep ourselves open for these spiritual interactions.

Through Jesus, God has shown us how to develop our connection and friendship with him. Practicing religion is the process by which we learn to communicate on a spiritual level. There are many different ways to reach this goal. Communal worship and prayers of petition connect us to God. Meditative prayer can open us to listen to God's word and receive his support. We are all part of God's family through the mystical body of Christ, but as in our families of origin, there are degrees of participation and support.

We tend to model the type of participation we learned in our family of origin. It is there that we learned how to communicate with God and our spiritual family. By observing family interactions, we have transferred what we have lived and learned to our image of God. Since our early minds could not think in abstract, we needed a mental picture of God and his family.

If Dad was strict and unyielding, our vision of God was a punishing God. Remember Frances? Her image of God was strict, powerful, and unbending. Her early environment encouraged this vision.

If our primary caregiver was easygoing, our first image of God was probably relaxed and laid-back. Usually as a child, our perception of God was masculine and father-like, probably because fathers were considered the head of the household. Our images of God may be strict, loving, compromising, permissive, caring, or fearful, depending on our early family experiences. As we age, we develop the ability to think abstractly, acquire knowledge, and experience relationships outside the family. These cause our perceptions to change.

FOR REFLECTION

❧ What were your early impressions of God?

❧ Are they still the same, or have they changed?

❧ How have they changed?

❧ How do you feel about the change?

Our spiritual friendships can include not only our relationship with God, but also with God's family—those who have gone before us and now live in God. These are not only the publicly acknowledged saints, but also members of our family or friends whom we now believe are living in God's glory. These suprapersonal relationships can be greatly enhanced by our reading and study of the scriptures, Jesus' life on earth, and our church's teachings. Quiet inner time provides the environment for contemplation of what we study. Over the years, our spiritual sensitivity may have become rusty; we may be bored with our spiritual conversations. We need to polish our contemplative skills and allow our souls to soar. Here are a few suggestions to begin the process:

❧ Plan some quiet time to open the door to spiritual connection. Talk to God frequently throughout the day.

❧ Learn about God through church teachings, scriptures, and life experiences. Apply his teachings to your everyday life.

❧ Celebrate life and make memories to realize God's precious gift of life.

Memories are an important part of our lives. We differ from the rest of the animal kingdom as we can remember the past and project into the future. What we see, hear, touch, taste, or smell becomes part of us. It forms pleasant or unpleasant memories. Your feelings about friendship with God will be influenced by memories you have created in your interpersonal relationships.

Exercise

As we age, memories become more precious. We cling to them more and more as short-term memory begins to fade and long-term memories take hold. Take a few minutes to relax. Travel back through your life. Think of a memory that is special to you.

- ❦ What makes this memory special to you?
- ❦ Who is involved? What is happening?
- ❦ What feelings are you experiencing as you bring this memory into the present?
- ❦ How does it relate to your spiritual life?
- ❦ What memories do you think others will have about you?
- ❦ What can you do that will form happy memories for your loved ones?

10
Communing Together

Communication enables us to connect with others. When we think about communication, we often think first of words. Although words are important, communicating is more than just using words. Besides the language of our words, there is the language of our bodies. Body language sends a message. The more congruency we have between these two dimensions, the more effective our communication will be.

Marge was aware that her daughter Helen was having difficulty with her teenage daughter Danielle. Danielle was actively rebelling against her parents and teachers. She was involved with questionable friends and had recently been involved in shoplifting. Marge wanted to talk to Helen about Danielle. She felt Helen was at fault for being too busy to be there for Danielle. Marge pondered how to discuss this delicate subject with her daughter. Here are three ways she might have gone about it. Which conversation feels most comfortable to you?

> "Helen, I need to talk to you. You never pay attention to Danielle. No wonder she is in trouble. You never paid attention to what I was saying, and it looks like you have not learned a thing."

or

> "You never should have had children. You are only
> concerned about yourself. In my day, you never
> would have gone to work and left the children. What
> is this world coming to?"

or

> "I'm concerned about Danielle. She seems so unhap-
> py. What do you think is happening in her life to
> make her act out as she is doing? How can I help?"

The first conversation triggers rejection. There is unfinished business from the past that Marge and Helen have not
resolved. The statements are directed toward Helen and attack her self-image. The second conversation labels Helen
selfish. How can she feel worthwhile when a significant person in her life implies she has abandoned her child?

The third conversation shows Marge's concern for her
granddaughter and deals with the problem at hand without
attacking Helen's self-esteem. Did you notice that the first
two conversations use the word "you," putting Helen on defense? In the third conversation, Marge uses the word "I." She
talks about her feelings and asks how she can help. A comfortable environment is created for problem solving.

These conversations emphasize the need to respect the
other's self-esteem in communication. Listening is another
important skill needed to communicate effectively. Most of us
do not appreciate our physical hearing ability until we begin
to lose it as we age or due to an injury or illness that has
caused hearing loss.

Janet's husband Paul has had a hearing loss that was
slightly noticeable early in their marriage. After serving two
years in the army, more nerve damage occurred and he became totally deaf in one ear. Paul did remarkably well in the
business field for many years. But as he aged, the hearing loss
became worse in his good ear. Janet noticed a strain in their
marriage as Paul begin to draw more and more into himself,

his self-image lowering as he couldn't hear conversations. Janet found herself talking loudly, almost bringing anger into her voice at times, as she became frustrated with trying to communicate with him. Paul's hearing disability rippled out to family and friends and inward to himself.

While physical inability or difficulty in hearing can certainly be an obstacle to communication, there is also the issue of listening. Each of us processes what we hear according to our life experiences. We tend to hear what we want to hear, not what is being said. When this occurs, our response is colored by our assumptions, not reality. For effective listening, be attentive to the person speaking. Wait five seconds before responding so you can become focused. Repeat back what you heard, asking for clarification if you need it. Respond with your thoughts using "I" statements. By following these steps, you are better able to understand what someone is trying to communicate to you and to avoid assumptions that may or may not be what is conveyed.

How do you know if someone is listening to you? Eye contact is important, but it does not assure listening is happening. They could be looking right at you and be thinking about something else. Body language sends signals for us to read. When I give workshops and lectures, I focus on the body language of the participants. Bodies that are too relaxed with closing eyes tell me that I need to perk up the lecture with a story or attention-getting tactics. Bodies that are too tense or fidgety signal a lack of comfort with the environment. A room that is too hot or too cold, chairs that are too hard, or loud background noises interfere with comfort and are distracting.

Exercise

Stand in front of a full length mirror and imagine you are talking to a friend. Express disappointment, then anger, then fear, and finally excitement.

❦ Do your facial and body expressions portray these feelings?

❦ Now try the same expressions with words. Do they match? If so, you are communicating your message effectively.

When you have something important to say or plan to talk for a period of time, get comfortable at eye level. Eye level contact creates comfort in communicating, as this exercise will demonstrate:

Exercise

Stand next to a partner who is sitting down. Begin a conversation, then after a few minutes switch places and continue talking.

❦ How did you feel standing while carrying on a conversation with someone sitting down?

❦ Did you feel in control or uncomfortable looking down?

❦ Did you want to sit down?

❦ How did you feel sitting down while your partner was standing and talking to you? Did you feel out of control, powerless?

❦ Did body parts begin to ache?

❦ Did you try to stand up to be on an equal level?

❦ Were you eager to end the conversation?

Try not to be judgmental while you are listening. Listen and answer back in a supportive manner that will open communication rather than close a conversation. "You sound upset that I didn't call to let you know where I was," instead of, "It's my business where I go, not yours."

When we listen, we hear not only the words that are spoken, but the meaning "between the lines." This type of listening requires that we let go of our need to formulate an answer before the person has finished speaking. Planning your answer interferes with concentrated listening.

Sometimes, no matter how hard we try to focus, our minds wander. Have you ever found yourself at Mass, perhaps even during the consecration, thinking about the handsome man sitting in front of you, wondering if he is single, and then feeling guilty? You are sure that no one else could ever have such thoughts at such a time. When we drift away because of lack of attention, we can call ourselves back, and if necessary, admit our lapse and ask for the speaker to repeat.

In speaking, use words that give positive outcomes. Instead of negative statements like, "Don't do that," "Can't you hear?" or "Can't you do anything right?" try, "It's time to . . ." "I would like you to help with this," or "This is an easier way to do this."

Stay away from labeling others or judging groups of people. See them as individuals. Labeling attacks self-esteem; talk about the action instead of the person. Try, "This meat is not cooked enough," instead of, "You can't cook."

Be generous with words of praise. Praise encourages us to try again, to feel we are pleasing others. Praise is recognition of achievements or effort. If you have difficulty praising or receiving a compliment, you may have some guarded feelings that need to be worked through. You may be trying too hard to protect your boundaries with feelings of jealousy and envy.

Carla was the oldest of six brothers and sisters. She had been an only child for five years before the others were born. Carla struggled all through her childhood for the affection of her parents. She learned to get this attention by following not only the spoken rules of the family, but unspoken ones as well. Praise wasn't given simply for doing the expected. She protected her boundaries with jealous feelings if attention was given to the other siblings by pointing out their faults or what they didn't do. She continued this behavior with her adult relationships.

Praise needs to be sincere. It can be given sincerely even if the outcome was a failure. It's nice to hear, "You worked hard on that diet. Do you realize how difficult it is to stick with a diet? How can I help?"

When something happens that bothers you, say the word "I" first. This will help you express your feelings and not put others on the defensive. Your feelings are your own and are not debatable. Beginning statements with "I" prevents labeling and name-calling. It allows feelings to be expressed without confrontation. After expressing your feelings, move on with a plan of action to solve the problem. Stay away from "You make me . . ." "You never . . ." and "You always . . ." statements that put the blame on others. Blaming others avoids accepting responsibility for your actions. "You" leaves others with no recourse other than involvement in a power struggle. Resolution becomes impossible.

For example, if one of your friends, whom you like very much, has the unfortunate habit of constantly interrupting you when you're right in the middle of a sentence, instead of grinning and bearing it, tell her you have a concern you'd like to share with her. "When I am interrupted in the middle of a sentence, I feel frustrated because I lose my thought process. How can we work this out?"

Or suppose you just found out your daughter and her family are moving away. You feel devastated and depressed. You are concerned about being alone. Here's a way to let her know how much you'll miss her without triggering guilt feelings. "I feel sad that you are moving because I'll miss you all so much. I'll feel better when we can plan how often we can visit each other."

Using "I" expresses your feelings, "when" states the situation and "because" gives a reason. This opens communication for a solution without lowering self-esteem.

If our words communicate love, concern, encouragement, acceptance, and understanding, we will be contributing to building strong connections in our relationships. By avoiding ridicule, sarcasm, rejection, annoyance, and impatience, we can nurture self-esteem in ourselves and others. This is what the psalmist means when he extols the virtue of "speaking truth from the heart."

FOR REFLECTION

What does "speaking truth from the heart" mean to you? Give an example of a situation in a relationship where you spoke from your heart. What was the outcome?

11
Changes in Relationships

The Queen in *Snow White and the Seven Dwarfs* had obstacles to overcome as she aged. Although she went about meeting these obstacles in a violent manner that finally destroyed her, she tried to keep what she wanted— youth, power, and beauty.

Living life during our older years means confronting the changes that occur in our relationships that may prevent us from fulfilling our needs and wants. As we age, we have different challenges to conquer than in earlier years.

The term "empty nest" has been associated with children leaving home as they reach adulthood. I'd like to expand this concept to include divorce or the death of a spouse. The term "changing nest" encompasses the various changes and challenges that pertain to aging in families that we will examine in this chapter.

LEARNING TO BE ALONE

When we are alone in the nest, we face many challenges to growth: powerful emotions, difficulties holding on to our self-esteem, and concerns about aging. We drive though our feelings like pot-holes on the road as we grieve the loss of our relationships and come face to face with our mortality.

Often the dominant feeling is one of loneliness. Loneliness is a painful emotion; it leaves us empty and depressed. Jesus experienced this agony in the Garden of Gethsemane. He felt lonely and abandoned, knowing what was ahead of him. Luke's gospel tells us: "And to strengthen him, an angel from heaven appeared to him. He was in such agony and he prayed so fervently that his sweat became like drops of blood falling on the ground" (Lk 22:43-45).

Being lonely and being alone are two different concepts. Loneliness is an emotional state of being; aloneness is a physical state of being. This explains why we can be surrounded by people, even those we care for very much, and still feel lonely. If we have not worked through self-image issues of conditional love and unworthiness, we can be lonely indeed. If our life has been lived through another person and that person leaves us or dies, we are lonely.

Roberta had been married 48 years when her husband died. He had been ill for a while and needed constant care. Roberta's life was enveloped in the care of her husband and her children. She kept house, cooked, did laundry, and set out her husband's clothes every morning. Roberta had a few friends, but no hobbies or interests except her family. Now her children were grown and living on their own, and she had lost her husband. She was indeed lonely. Eleven years later, when her family insisted she have counseling, she was still grieving, willing herself to die to be with her husband. She refused to help herself, withdrew more and more into herself, and finally drifted into death.

When our nest changes and we are alone, it is time to extend our family by changing family patterns, nurturing old friendships, and reaching out to form new connections. Being physically alone can boost self-image. We need time to be alone to think and to sort out life. As I grow older I find I cherish quiet and stillness. Time alone enables me to observe and appreciate nature and to see the beauty of my surroundings that I have taken for granted. I have created little patches of beauty in my home and yard to draw me into retreat and peace. Time is more precious to me as I age. I am more selective about how my time is spent.

To be able to accept changes in life, we need to look inward for regrouping. Looking deeply into ourselves presents questions that need to be answered. What do I do now? Where do I go from here? What support do I need and how will I get it?

Another roadblock we run into is the feeling of uselessness that is sometimes triggered by loneliness. Our responsibilities have changed, and we are forced to move to another stage in life. Without a clear sense of what our new responsibilities are, we can fall into a sense of being useless. Only by being creative as we age can we move beyond these feelings. By recognizing present patterns and creating new ones, it is easier to accept the changes. It's time to challenge old expectations and take risks to develop realistic ones to fit our new lifestyle. Our attitudes will become more positive, we'll learn to see the extraordinary in the ordinary, and we'll take advantage of the unexpected to enliven our day. The changing nest will not be so scary or lonely if we can accept aloneness as growth.

LEARNING TO BE TOGETHER

As we age, relationships present us with new challenges. Whether we are with our longtime spouse, recently married, or living with a friend, there are changes to be negotiated. The challenge of aloneness and the feeling of loneliness can confront us even if we are making this transition in the company of others. We must relearn how to be together. If after some time being single we begin a new relationship with a spouse or share our home with a relative or friend, the new relationship will present us with new challenges. While in the past our relational lives may have been strained by a lack of time with our partner, now there may be too much togetherness. Underlying problems that in the past were ignored because of family needs and work outside the home are now visible and nagging.

Those of us who are making this transition with our spouse may discover that we may have grown apart. We may be strangers to each other. We wait for comfortable feelings to happen before we act kindly to each other instead of doing actions that encourage growth in our relationship.

Regardless of how our relationships have changed, this is the time to care for and be cared for gently. Practice caring behavior whether it feels comfortable or not. By doing at least one planned caring action a day, you can begin to change your behavior and reap the positive results. A written message such as a "thank you" or a simple "I love you" placed on your partner's pillow can start the process. Take the responsibility to let your partner know what caring actions you appreciate. Acknowledge the things done for you. Keep a list of the activities you are doing that enhance the relationship.

Communication issues seem to be the most obvious challenge. Many of us have difficulty with conflict resolution. Poor conflict resolution skills obstruct relationships. We don't know how to "fight fair." It is easy to carry all our baggage from years of marriage and to want to continually dump on our partner. We know which button to push that puts the other on defense.

Here are some helpful ground rules for resolving conflicts:

- ❧ Use "I" statements to talk about your feelings. Stay away from "You" statements which put the blame on your partner;

- ❧ Use How, What, and Where questions instead of Why;

- ❧ No labeling, name calling, or finger pointing;

- ❧ Deal with here and now issues. The past is over and cannot be changed;

- ❧ Take responsibility for a settlement;

- ❧ Use problem solving techniques. Pinpoint the problem by identifying facts. Express your opinions in a non-threatening manner and brainstorm actions for solutions. Compromise if a consensus can not be reached;

❦ When feelings are out of control, take time out to manage them. Set a time to continue communication for a solution;

❦ Stay away from button-pushing techniques such as crying, screaming, walking away, storing feelings, and dumping them;

❦ Be assertive, but do not intrude on the other person or on yourself;

❦ Attitudes such as dominance, competitiveness, superiority or submissiveness hinder conflict resolution. They are manipulative and lead to playing games.

Sometimes games have been played for so long that they are hardly recognizable. The game "You decide" is one that is often played:

"Honey, what would you like to do tonight? We could go to a movie or visit Tom and Susan."

"I don't know. Either is fine."

"Well which would you rather do?"

"I don't care."

"Can't you ever make a decision?"

"What do you mean? I'll do either. You decide."

And so it goes on and on. Another common game is to have a guessing game progressing.

"Did you get to the store?"

"Yep."

"What did you buy?"

"Oh, nothing much."

"Did you see Arnie?"

"Yep."

"Well, what did he say?"

"Nothing much."

Getting information is like playing twenty questions.

When we play communication games, we do not take responsibility for communicating clearly: owning our own feelings, speaking assertively, discussing the issue, compromising, and moving to a solution.

Exercise

Try this with your partner to improve your communicating skills. Take turns completing the following statements:

- ❦ Something that bothers me is . . .
- ❦ I feel hurt when . . .
- ❦ One thing I feel angry about is . . .
- ❦ I enjoy when . . .
- ❦ One thing I appreciate is . . .
- ❦ I am pleased with our relationship when . . .

Answer each of these statements by repeating what you have heard.

- ❦ I hear you saying . . .

Ask for clarification if you need it. Then respond with how you feel about what was said using "I" statements.

INTIMACY

The highest level of communication in a relationship is intimacy. Intimacy is a body and soul connection that leads us into the spiritual dimension. Like a fine wine, to taste the fullness of intimacy takes aging. Sex is one way of expressing intimacy. Sexual love evolves and moves through stages of growth. Society models only the excitable stage of attraction that we experienced so intently when we were young. Sex is used to sell everything from cars to washing machines. It is financially beneficial. However, such of view of sexuality denies aging. It fragments the natural process of life from birth to death by focusing on one development stage, youth. The mirrors presented to us are distorted and our reflections incongruent with where we are in life.

When sex and love are wedded, intimacy can blossom into wholeness. The first stage of chemical attraction is pleasurable and necessary to pollinate the flower of love. Then there is a settling in, allowing comfort and growth to germinate. Nurturing is important for the seed of love to sprout. The stage of distraction then occurs in mid-life as we question who we are and what we want. This stage creates couple problems and requires a willingness to make adjustments to get through these difficulties. Finally, we settle into a mutual comfort zone of intimate communication. What is important is mutual agreement and commitment.

Sex is only one of many forms of human intimacy. The greatest form of intimacy we know is the Trinity. The Father, Son, and Holy Spirit are fused by love into one being, an intimacy that is total and complete. As we age, the physical action of intercourse may be replaced by caring touches and actions. If we feel good about ourselves and the one we love, we do not have to prove ourselves sexually. We just need to love and be loved.

George and Betty had been married for 35 years. They found themselves with different interests and quarreled over the smallest points. Their children were grown and on their own, so they agreed to live separately. During this separation, George had an affair. Betty was devastated.

As we worked together in counseling, it became evident that they still cared for each other and were committed to the marriage. Affairs usually are symptoms of problems in a marriage. George's self-image was threatened as he aged. He saw Betty aging, her figure changing, her hair graying, and her interests changing. This was the mirror in which he was seeing his reflection. George appeared outgoing, wanting to do youthful activities, and was working to keep physically fit. But in spite of appearances to others, his self-esteem was low. He buried his fear of aging.

Betty became passive-aggressive as she realized she didn't want to keep up with George's determination to stay young. She let herself go physically, which gave George the permission he was looking for to have an affair with a younger woman. My job was to help George uncover his fear of aging and to help Betty feel better about herself. As they worked on themselves, the marriage began to improve and the trust issue became workable.

RETIREMENT

Retirement is another passage in life that challenges us. Whether we retire from a career or from family responsibilities, it denotes change in our lives. Concerns and questions arise. Who am I now that my responsibilities have changed? What do I do with the rest of my life? How will I survive on a limited income? Where should I live?

If your work has been the sole source of your self-image, you will feel at a loss. Our generation in particular has defined our self-image by working roles. We need to separate self from work. We need to look deep into ourselves to find out who we are. Take time to get to know yourself.

FOR REFLECTION

- ❦ What kind of person am I? (Values)
- ❦ What are my best assets?
- ❦ Do I accept responsibility for my actions?
- ❦ How do I accept change?
- ❦ Do I love unconditionally?
- ❦ Am I committed to relationships?
- ❦ Am I flexible in my decision-making?
- ❦ Do I have a sense of humor?
- ❦ Where am I going?

Now that we are living longer, retirement needs to be re-framed. We need to think of retirement as change, a beginning rather than an ending. It is a time to pursue interests and activities we have always wanted to do, but never had the time to do. It is the time we have planned and worked to reach.

Jesus asked St. Peter to give up his work of fishing and become a "fisher of men." What a difficult decision this must have been for him, to give up the only work he knew how to do! He must have pondered his decision. How would he be able to support his family if he left them to follow Jesus? How could he be a fisher of men? He had no skills. What would others think of him? He took the risk.

Digging into our past for interests and activities we enjoyed and setting goals for ourselves can help the transition into retirement. This is one time taking risks can pay off. Learning to play a musical instrument, learning a new language, attending cooking classes, developing a herb garden, or volunteering at a hospital involve risk but help us move on in life.

For our forty-first wedding anniversary, our children arranged for us to take a hot-air balloon ride. It was a complete surprise with no time to think about it. If I would have thought about it, I probably would have made many excuses not to take the ride. What an experience I would have missed! I saw the world in a different light. We floated in space, able to view our ranch and the surrounding areas. We had a look at God's creation from a different perspective. I felt the thrill of a new experience that nurtured the child in me.

Money can be another challenge to our relationships. It plays such an important role in our lives; we cannot escape the power it has over us. Lowering our standard of living is difficult. Trying to "down size" because of limited income can attack our self-esteem. Basic needs of food, shelter, and clothing become pronounced. These commodities are costly today. We want to keep our independence as we age, but we need to be creative about ways to keep our comfort.

Preparing financially for retirement is a must. Whether we find ourselves forcefully or voluntarily retired, we still need to prepare. A friend, family member, or community service can help us assess our finances. Assets, pensions, and social security benefits should all be examined. These areas of finance can be especially difficult for older women. We were raised with expectations that these needs would be taken care of by our husbands. Our work as housewives would be rewarded financially. We would live happily ever after. We had no need to prepare for the unexpected.

As we down-size, we question where to live. Most older women must rely on their own ingenuity to supplement their income after the death of their partner. Selling a home, leaving family and friends, health, and climate are factors in determining what to do. A written inventory of pros and cons is one tool that may help the decision-making process.

OUR ADULT CHILDREN

Relating to our adult children who may have families of their own can be another challenge. The transition from the mother-child relationship to a mutually respected adult relationship is difficult to achieve. We need to develop a connecting adult friendship with our children. We have moved from a dependency relationship to recognition of each other as separate personalities that need to be mutually respected. Skills are needed to facilitate this process.

Communication that does not put our children on the defensive is necessary. Our children need open, honest communication that does not carry baggage with it. If there is no conflict resolution, compromise is effective. Asking for clarification of what we do not understand gives us an advantage in communicating.

Setting new family goals as the family becomes more extended enlightens members on where they fit in and where they are going. Values will change as we find ourselves the oldest generation. These changes may create crises that we can grow from if we open ourselves up to the changes.

Becoming grandparents opens new avenues in our parenting skills. We are not the parents of these children and may feel out of control in establishing a relationship with our grandchildren that does not intrude on our children's responsibility of child rearing. Planning special time alone with each grandchild is not only rewarding for us, it will also leave memories for them. Enlarging on their interests by day-long excursions, traveling, or dinner out makes them feel special and helps us to have that quality time that develops a relationship. As we age, we need quality time with each member of our extended family. Reunions are one way to keep in touch, but many times they are hectic or difficult to make happen.

Our Aging Parents

Caring for aging parents can be a difficult challenge, yet it has its rewards. As our parents become more childlike and dependent on us, we become more parentlike. By helping them celebrate their winter years, we learn to celebrate our aging. Yet they present us with serious concerns and decisions to make.

What is it like to have parents growing old and frail? We have more responsibilities as their needs increase. We see them as mirrors that reflect our mortality. Our feelings and emotions are up and down. The feeling of sadness overwhelms us as we see our once strong and invincible parents so weak and helpless. We may lash out in anger, hiding our guilt over what we should or shouldn't have done for them. Our parents, in most cases, did much for us when we were helpless children. We feel we owe them our lives.

We punish ourselves with self-talk that triggers guilt because they are so needy and demand so much from us. "My parents took care of me when I was helpless and dependent; now I should take care of them." But in some cases, we do not have the capability to give the professional care that may be needed. Yet we feel guilt if we have to turn them over to others for care.

How do our parents feel about growing old? Some have maintained vigor and remain in the mainstream of life with good health, interests, friends, and loving relationships. For others, growing old means loss—of physical health, job, friends, and pleasure. They withdraw gradually from living, feeling isolated and lonely.

Society today views old age as burdensome. There is a great push for youth. Not too long ago, the elderly were a small portion of the population. They lived in rural communities and had tasks to do. Urban growth changed all this as families became mobile. The elderly were stripped of their identity, of their roles of spouses, workers, and parents. They were locked into loneliness. Corporations moved families far away from home. Modular living did not make room for an extended family. As a result, government agencies, programs, and nursing homes were established to care for the elderly.

What options do we have? Concerns need to be discussed openly and frankly in an assertive manner. Try to reach a joint decision, considering the needs of each member of the family. Help aging parents keep their self-esteem by considering their basic physical needs, affection, freedom, and independence.

We need to keep our aging parents comfortable and independent for as long as possible. This means evaluating their situation regularly. Multiple supports may be needed to help them remain on their own for as long as possible. This will help them feel they are not disappearing behind a closed door, slipping into loneliness.

If finances or health do not permit parents to live alone, and you choose to have them move in with you, be sure all arrangements are discussed thoroughly beforehand. Issues of money, chores, furniture, meals, and living space need to be considered with respect for all family members.

If you decide on care away from home, investigate the numerous options from limited care to complete care. This research is important; contact agencies and learn all you can. With this input and an understanding of what you are able to do, an informed decision can be made.

GRIEVING

Facing our mortality can be the most difficult challenge of all. Mortality issues involve grieving and affect relationships. As our friends and family members become terminally ill and die, we come face to face with an awareness of our own impending death. Awareness of our own mortality gives a crisp intensity to each moment we experience. We see things around us that we ignored before. The trees look more beautiful, the sunsets more spectacular, and the butterflies more free. We become like little children seeing the world through new glasses. We become more childlike as we live each precious moment.

Looking through the eyes of faith can help us to uncover our fears of death. We need to work through the experiences of death that affect our relationships with ourselves, others, and God. It becomes important to develop friendships with people of all ages so as not to find ourselves alone as our peers die.

FOR REFLECTION

- How do you feel about aging and dying?
- How did you feel when you lost a loved one to death?
- How old were you when you experienced death in another for the first time?
- Which experience was most traumatic for you? Why?
- How long do you expect to live?
- What are your fears about death?
- What past regrets do you have?
- How would you have done things differently?

When Marsha turned 60, she was devastated. Her birthday was nothing to celebrate. After two weeks of depression, she decided she would fight getting old. She bought a new convertible. She made an appointment for plastic surgery to remove any signs of wrinkles on her face. She booked a cruise on the "love boat." Marsha lost herself in activities to delay the time when she would have to process her attitudes on aging. She lapsed back into depression when these Band-Aids did not heal the fear of old age and dying.

We grieve for our lost youth. If we have been dependent on images of ourselves provided by society's mirrors, aging becomes difficult. The Queen in *Snow White and the Seven Dwarfs* is a powerful symbol of old age. We see her type repeated in other story characters such as the Sea Witch in *The Little Mermaid* or the old lady in *Hansel and Gretel*. They all deny becoming old, either by killing or stealing the youth of another. Note how the Queen will not face her loss of youth:

> And when she had dressed herself in beautiful clothes, she went to her looking glass and said, "Mirror, mirror on the wall, who is fairest of them all?" The looking glass answered "O Queen, although you are of beauty rare, the young princess is a thousand times more fair." Then she railed and cursed and was beside herself with disappointment and anger (*Grimm's Household Stories*).

Losing ones we love is the greatest pain of loss we can experience. The pain is deep, stomach crunching. It must be a sample of the pain of loss we would experience if we were denied access to God.

Our values about aging and mortality are developed from our feelings about these experiences of loss. The grieving process needs to be experienced for us to feel whole again. When we realize someone is mortally ill, we go into shock. The body's defense is denial. "This is not happening," we say. This is why burial rituals help us accept the obvious and move through denial.

Our feelings become all encompassing as we move on in the grieving stage. There is anger. It can be directed at God for being so cruel to let this happen, or it can be directed at the

person for leaving us. It may even be directed at ourselves—
"If only I would have done something else, this would have
not happened." The anger covers up other feelings that need
to be explored and dealt with, such as hurt that we are left
alone, fear of our own mortality, or depression as we turn inward in despair.

We try various methods to help us through these feelings.
Bargaining is one. We fast or pray novenas, anything to prevent this illness or circumstance from happening. We bargain
with God: "If you help me, I'll do something for you." When
we do not get the results we want, we blame God. We may
even lose our faith.

As we heal over time, we reach acceptance and can begin to move on in our lives. Keep in mind that there is no
time limit on grieving. When we lose a loved one, we continue to move in and out of all the stages of grief. As time
passes, the intensity lessens. The power to heal emotionally
is within us, just as the ability to heal physically is. The pain
lessens as we reach out to others who have experienced a
similar situation. The following is a comforting meditation
that has helped me work through my pain of loss.

Comfort for Those Who Mourn

*So many people imagine that death cruelly separates us from
our loved ones. Even pious people are led to believe this great
and sad mistake. When our loved ones die, they do not leave us.
They remain. They do not go to some dark and distant place.
They simply begin their eternity. We do not see them because
we are still in the darkness of the world. But their spiritual eyes,
filled with the light of heaven, are always watching us as they
wait for the day when we shall share their perfect joy. We are all
born for heaven and one by one we end this life of tears to begin
our life in endless happiness.*

*I have often reflected upon this beautiful truth and found it the
greatest and surest comfort in time of mourning. A firm faith in
the real and continual presence of our loved ones has not destroyed them, nor carried them away. Rather it has given them*

life! A life with power to know fully and to love perfectly. With this new life and new power our loved ones are always present to us, knowing and loving us more than ever before.

The tears that dampen our eyes in times of mourning are tears of homesickness, tears of longing for our loved ones. But it is we who are away from home, not they. Death has been for them a doorway to an eternal home. And only because this heavenly home is invisible to our worldly eyes, we cannot see them so near us. Yet, they are with us, lovingly and tenderly waiting for the day when we, too, will enter the doorway of our eternal home. No, death is not a separation. It is a preparation for eternal union with those we love, in the peace and joy of heaven.

—Author Unknown

Mortality concerns are affected by our relationship with God. What we believe about God determines how we communicate with him. If we are on an acquaintance level, we remain in the denial stage of the relationship. Life becomes a goal in itself. We live life, not because of the miraculous gift it is, but because of the impending termination of life. If we are on a friendship level, our spiritual relationship will be on the bargaining level. We use prayers of petition to ask for wants and needs. When we form an intimate relationship with God, we experience acceptance and submit to God willingly.

Relationships are integral parts of us. Whether they are intrapersonal, interpersonal, or suprapersonal, they complete our human nature. We desire long-lasting, fulfilling relationships. Skills are the tools needed to build our connections to others.

FOR REFLECTION

Read Psalm 15 again. Take time to reflect on its meaning to your life.

Lord, who may abide in your tent?
Who may dwell on your holy mountain?
Whoever works without blame,

doing what is right,
speaking truth from the heart;
Who does not slander a neighbor,
does no harm to another,
never defames a friend;
Who disdains the wicked,
but honors those who fear the Lord;
Who keeps an oath despite the cost,
lends no money at interest,
accepts no bribe against the innocent.
Whoever acts like this
shall never be shaken.

—Psalm 15

❦ How are your intrapersonal, interpersonal, and suprapersonal relationships connected to this psalm?

❦ List strengths in your present friendships with family and friends.

❦ What needs improvement?

❦ What similarities do you see in your spiritual relationship with God?

Part III

Freedom to Be Me

12
To Be Free of . . .

Maturity is a time of life to take inventory, to be free of the old and move on to the new. Taking an inventory of our life will no doubt place us in touch with our expectations. When we examined the issue of expectations in Chapter 6, we focused on developing realistic expectations for our state in life and meeting them. In this chapter we'll look at how we can let go of unrealistic expectations that we carry from the past and become more free.

Unfulfilled past expectations may collide with our present expectations and create conflict for us. Yet conflicts are the stuff of growth; they just need to be worked through.

Freedom balances conflicts as we move from past expectations to present expectations. To be free means to "let go." It enables us to make unencumbered decisions about our lives. Unrealistic expectations prevent us from "letting go" and moving on. We need to challenge expectations we have held on to that hinder us from growing as we age. It may well be that these are unrealistic expectations.

Letting Go

The expectation that we need to be loved and approved by everyone for everything we do is unrealistic. It prevents us from being who we are. We shut ourselves down and become prisoners of others. Instead we should remove masks and let our real selves shine through. Yes, we need to be approved by others, especially those who mean the most to us. This is a desirable goal to achieve. But when it is achievable only at the expense of ourselves, we need to re-evaluate and let go. Strive to do what you enjoy and want to do in life without injuring yourself or others.

Let go of the expectation of being completely competent and achieving at all times. Perfectionism prevents us from living life fully. Separate being from doing. You can strive to be a better cook, but that won't make you a better person. Attaining your performance goal will enhance your self-image and put you on the course of self-esteem, but if you expect to be perfect and you fail, you may not feel good enough about yourself to try again.

Being perfect does not allow room for taking risks. The fear of failure is frightening for perfectionists. Making mistakes is not allowed. But when we learn from our mistakes, we grow. Expecting perfection in ourselves is unrealistic and results in frustration. Expecting perfection in others hampers connecting with them. Relationships are strained.

Nothing in life is perfect: a beautiful rose has a brown spot; a new dress has a pulled thread; it rains on the day of your well-planned luncheon. Acknowledge that there are circumstances beyond your control. Plan for them. Life does not always follow the path you would like. When conditions are not the way you would like them to be, try to change them for the better. If they cannot be changed at present, be patient and accepting until something can be done.

Separate behavior from character. The expectation that our identity is based on what we do rather than who we are can be misleading. We may not like what others do, but we need to recognize all living creatures as God's creation. Stay away from blaming others for their actions. Perhaps if we stepped into their shoes, we would behave in the same way. Instead of blaming others, examine your own behavior. In non-threatening ways, plan how to change behavior that is under your control to make it socially acceptable.

We can let go of the expectation that happiness is "an end in itself." Maturity cements the concept that "things" do not make happiness. All of us can relate to incidents of wanting something more than anything else. "If only I can have that new car or that new bedroom set or that beautiful new dress, I'll be so happy and not want another thing." After we acquire the object, the novelty wears off and we do want something else. Happiness is the by-product of our self-esteem, not of things. When we feel loved and valuable, we are happy.

To be free to grow, we need to let go of fears that interfere with our lives. We all have fears of one sort or another. Problems exist when fears take over our lives. Assess what fears you have. If they are disrupting your life, work to erase them. Study them. The more we know about our fears, the less threatening they become. Find out what alternatives you have. Get help if you need it. Phobias are treatable. When a fear is stopping you from doing what you want to do, it is time to get help.

Annie is afraid of flying. Now that her husband Ed is retired, he wants to travel. They have a condo in Arizona so they can get away from the damp winters in Seattle. Driving is too exhausting for them. Ed found himself going alone because Annie could not get on the plane. She would be packed to go, and at the last minute, crying and trembling, she would back out. This was causing friction in her marriage and unhappiness in her life. She felt out of control. Ed suggested she get help through a phobia clinic. She refused, saying it would do no good. It was a standoff.

ACCEPTING RESPONSIBILITY

Maturity helps us to accept responsibilities. The expectation that we will be rescued from responsibility to live "happily ever after" is not realistic. We should be able to accept our responsibilities, not run from them or place them on others. There's no prince coming to rescue us. We need to rescue ourselves. Coming to that realization may be shocking. At this time in our lives, there may be no one to help us but ourselves. We need to set our sights for expectations that determine what we can do and what help we truly need to meet our responsibilities.

In order to accept responsibilities, we need to be self-disciplined. Self-discipline is freedom from disarray. It touches all aspects of our living. It is a considered plan for living usefully and happily with ourselves and others. Self-discipline allows us to have the ability to think for ourselves and make decisions accordingly. It is difficult to achieve, but much more rewarding than the undisciplined or easy way.

When we are self-disciplined, we have a more organized life. This means more time to do the things we want to do. Procrastination disappears in a self-disciplined environment. Self-discipline also enables us to manage our feelings in socially accepted ways. Our relationships become more open and honest. We have the freedom to be ourselves. Attaining self-discipline gives us peace of mind. There is comfort in the order of things, and we can become better at creating ourselves.

Letting go of the past is critical if we are to reframe the false expectation that all problems stem from our youth. The past is important and has impact on the present, but most problems we carry with us from the past to the present can be surrendered or worked through. Rethink and rework undesirable past habits into habits that will help you grow. Stay away from mantras like, "If only I had . . ." "I should (or shouldn't) have. . . ." Reframe these phrases in the present tense, "I will . . ." "I can. . . ."

Accept reality for what it is. We can wish things to be different, but we are powerless to change the grim realities of life. We learn in maturity that we need to compromise and accept reasonable solutions to crises and problems that occur. The better we feel about ourselves, the quicker we can bounce back from crisis.

Freedom is letting go of the expectation that we need friendships to be socially approved. Become interested in others for their own sake, not for what they can do for you. The number of friends we have is not as important as the quality of those friendships. A few good friends who are loyal and whose love is unconditional are valuable assets in life. Passivity does not develop such relationships; only with active involvement in our relationships can we achieve maximum happiness and fulfillment.

Letting go of expectations that hinder our growth will help us achieve freedom and become balanced. Develop goals that will help you create more balanced expectations. Be kind to yourself and others as you travel through life. Avoid needlessly hurting others as you fulfill your expectations, needs, and wants. Work diligently to implement your goals successfully. When you create balance and freedom in your life, your life will be pleasing to God and to yourself.

Nadine Stair has written her version of the popular phrase, "If I had my life to live over":

If I had my life to live over . . . I'd dare to make more mistakes next time. I'd relax, I would limber up. I would be sillier than I have been this trip. I would take fewer things seriously. I would take more chances. I would climb more mountains and swim more rivers. I would eat more ice cream and less beans. I would perhaps have more actual troubles, but I'd have fewer imaginary ones.

You see, I'm one of those people who live sensibly and sanely hour after hour, day after day. Oh, I've had my moments, and if I had it to do over again, I'd have more of them. In fact, I'd try to have nothing else. Just moments, one after another, instead of living so many years ahead of each day. I've been one of those persons who never goes anywhere without a thermometer, a hot water bottle, a raincoat and a parachute. If I had to do it again, I would travel lighter than I have.

If I had my life to live over, I would start barefoot earlier in the spring and stay that way later in the fall. I would go to more dances. I would ride more merry-go-rounds. I would pick more daisies. (*If I Had My Life to Live Over, I Would Pick More Daisies.* Edited by Sandra Halderman Martz. Freedom, CA: Papier-Mache Press.)

If you had your live to live over, what would you do?

13
Accomplishing Balance

To be in balance is to have a sense of proportion, discretion, and adjustment. In balance there is freedom from disarray. There is poise in the balance of life. God created the world in balance, with the right number of plants to feed the right number of animals. The right number of animals to fulfill human needs. God created the right amount of sunshine and water for life. Only humankind has disturbed this balance.

Psalm 136 celebrates the delicate balance of creation:

Praise the Lord of lords;
God's love endures forever;
Who skillfully made the heavens,
God's love endures forever;
Who spread the earth upon the waters,
God's love endures forever;
Who made the great lights,
God's love endures forever;
The sun to rule the day,
God's love endures forever;
The moon and stars to rule the night,
God's love endures forever.

—Psalm 136:3-10

God created us to be in balance. How do we keep this balance in our journey of life? Molly's granddaughter, Kimberly, has a whimsical mobile hanging in the corner of her room. This gift from Aunt Sue delighted her, and even though it has a Halloween theme, she has it displayed all year round. There is a witch flying on a broom, a black cat curiously watching her, a smiling pumpkin enjoying life, and a ghoulish white ghost trying to scare them all. They all float and move in space in perfect balance. During one of Molly's visits, Kimberly came running out of her room crying. Her little brother accidentally hit the mobile with a flying toy, and the ghost fell to the ground. The mobile tilted and was out of balance. Grandma came to the rescue, and the mobile was quickly swinging in balance again.

Keeping body and soul in balance through life's experiences is difficult to do. It takes planning, knowledge, and determination for successful balance. The results are well worth the effort, however. Wellness is a necessary requirement to living life fully.

PHYSICAL BALANCE

Prevention is the key to keeping our bodies in balance. Physical health opens the door to emotional and spiritual health. When we do not feel good or are out of sorts, it affects everything we think and do. As we age, it becomes more and more difficult to keep healthy as body parts wear down.

This is a period in life when we are interested and have time to study health. Knowledge is the first step in maintaining health. Now that our responsibilities of family and career are lightened, we can devote time to our well being. We also pass on our knowledge and experience to our grown children as mentors for their well-being.

Determination is necessary to stick with changing health plans. Diets may be difficult to stay with, but rewards can help. Medical treatments to make us more comfortable require consistency, and in many cases long-term commitment is necessary. Estrogen Replacement Therapy is an example, and there are reasons why women are not enamored with it. Life-long commitment to ERT is urged for the prevention of osteoporosis and heart attacks, but the fear of cancer looms on the horizon. Research is not conclusive and women are confused. The use of ERT is financially lucrative for its manufacturers, yet another reason why it is difficult to get proper input on how to be in charge of our bodies.

Healthy eating habits are crucial in the later years of life. Unfortunately, this is the time when we become lax, as we are tired of following dieting rules for so many years. Diet, exercise, fresh air, plenty of rest, and checkups help keep our energy levels up and are common sense.

Some diet-wise tips to increase energy and keep weight down after 50:

- Try not to skip meals. Eat lighter meals more often.
- Stay away from caffeine products as they give a high and then set you down. Try herbal teas.
- Drink lots of water and juices to replenish the fluids that tend to dry up as we age.
- Sugary or salty snacks add empty calories. Fresh and dried fruits give energy if you can eat them.
- Try to cook your own food or get help doing so rather than using canned and packaged products with high sodium.
- Eat protein rich, low-fat dairy products to build your body as well as to maintain it.
- Try to prevent constipation by filling up naturally with whole grain bread.

Of course, if your doctor has put you on a special diet, be sure to follow it. Remember, you are what you eat!

Rest is nourishing and energizing. As we age, we do not sleep as deeply as when we were young. We wake up more often. Hot flashes and full bladders add to our unrest. Because

we sleep fitfully during the night, we need to take rest periods
or "power naps" during the day.

Exercise

Try this approach to resting and becoming refreshed:

Lie down on your bed. Place a pillow under your head. Be
sure you tug it down to fit under your neck. Place a small pillow under your knees to keep the pressure off your lower
back. Place your hands on your stomach. Close your eyes.
Then, starting with your toes, press them together as tight as
you can for the count of five.

Relax for the count of five. Travel up your body tensing
and relaxing each part. Don't forget fingers, hands, and arms.
Be sure you keep breathing. Do not be concerned if you do
not sleep. Just relax. Think pleasant thoughts. Rest for at least
15 minutes. Do this once or twice a day when you feel tired
and slowed down.

If you have trouble falling asleep at night, after telling
God about your day, try the above approach to relax. If you
still cannot fall asleep after 20 minutes or so, get up and go
into another room. Sit in a comfortable chair and read until
you feel sleepy. Then try again to sleep in bed. If worries are
occupying your mind, keep a pencil and paper by your bed-
side and jot down those worries. Your mind will be free to let
go until morning.

Fresh air and exercise are important for relaxing. A walk to
enjoy the outdoors is not only good for physical health, but is
like sunshine for mental health. Problems seem a little lighter
as nature wraps herself around us. Walking is the oil we need
to loosen joints and muscles. As we age and use our bodies
less, muscles and joints seem to have a mind of their own. This
is especially noticeable in the morning when we try to get out
of bed. Our muscles and joints become stiff as we age and use
them less. It helps to limber up in bed for a few minutes before
standing up.

Exercise

Try this exercise in bed before getting up. It helps me to start my morning more comfortably:

Lying flat in bed, bend your right leg and bring your knee to your chest, clasping your leg with both hands while your left leg is straight. Hold that position for the count of five. Do the same with your left leg. Next bring both knees to your chest and hold for five seconds. Then repeat the whole exercise one more time. Repeat this exercise with both knees bent and feet flat on the bed. Now, keeping your knees bent, your feet and back flat on the bed, and your hands under your lower back, tighten your stomach muscles pushing your lower back to the bed and holding for five seconds. Repeat.

Next, stretch your arms above your head and keep your legs as straight as possible and stretch as long as you can. Relax and repeat. With your arms stretched out at right angles from your sides, slowly turn your head to the right, hold; then to the center, hold; then to the left, hold; and then to the center once again. Now you're ready to roll out of bed on your side. While standing, stretch up on your tiptoes with your arms straight up, trying to reach the ceiling. Then go limp. Repeat again. Now you're ready to move into your day.

Whatever exercise you choose to do is fine, as long as you do it regularly and do not overdo it. Walking seems to be the easiest exercise to be consistent with, and it strengthens bones. Walking, swimming, biking, or golfing all keep us feeling fit. Just dancing around the house to music gets you moving and feeling good. Cleaning house to music involves bending and stretching to rhythm and gets the house clean too. New research tells us just two or three ten-minute periods of physical exercise daily can keep us fit. What is important is to be up and moving, and to be consistent.

EMOTIONAL BALANCE

Accomplishing emotional balance takes awareness as feelings need to be sorted out. Feelings are intangible and difficult to grab hold of. Love is a powerful feeling that can tip out of balance easily. The uncertainties of conditional love may easily throw us out of balance. To get us back in balance, conditional love needs to be replaced with unconditional love. Start with yourself.

Seven Steps Toward Loving Yourself More

1. Love yourself, faults, blemishes, and all. Remember there is only one you in the world. You are unique.

2. Allow yourself to express feelings without guilt. You have a right to your feelings. They make up the human part of you. It's what we do with our feelings that we are held accountable for.

3. Get rid of pent-up anger in appropriate ways. Keep in mind we may not hurt ourselves, others, or property. Choose three ways you can release anger that are acceptable to you and others around you. If slamming doors is not acceptable to you, try punching a pillow.

4. Learn to care for your body and soul in the best way. They are woven together and can strengthen your emotional health.

5. Reward yourself for taking risks to add sparkle to your life.

6. Praise your accomplishments by doing something special for yourself.

7. Ask for hugs and acts of kindness from significant others if you are not getting them. Be sure to give caring acts to others to satisfy their needs as well as your need for feeling worthy.

To be balanced emotionally means to live in the present. It's all we have. The past is over. It cannot ever be relived. The future is unknown to us. We do not know how much future we have. Remembering the past sheds light on the present; planning for the future provides security in the present. Then let go.

Many times I find myself not living in the present moment. I decide to go for a walk. While I'm walking, my mind is pondering all I have to do. I shouldn't be walking; I should be making phone calls, planning what to make for dinner, or going to the post office. Instead of walking and enjoying my surroundings—the warm sun, the grass under my feet, sounds of birds, the leaves and flowers along the way—I am distracted and miss the beauty around me. I'm living in the future I do not have.

Exercise

Try this exercise which I use with myself and my clients to practice living in the present:

Sit in a chair. Wiggle in until you feel comfortable. Look around the room slowly. Then close your eyes. What can you remember seeing? What colors did you see? Listen attentively while your eyes are closed. What sounds do you hear? Now feel the parts of your body that are touching the chair. What parts are comfortable, what parts are not? Slowly open your eyes and remain in the present for a few more minutes, taking in the sights and sounds around you.

Living in the present gives us the freedom to experience life fully in the here and now. It keeps us in balance. Work helps us to achieve balance by helping us feel good about ourselves. It brings back the creativity we lost along the way of life. All of us are able to create in one way or another. Take time to explore your imagination for creativity and balance.

Exercise

Plan a project you have never done before. Be sure you choose something you always have wanted to do. Maybe it is learning to make a quilt or play the piano. Perhaps it's attending a pottery class to learn to make a vase. Take a risk and do it. Make greeting cards to send to your grandchildren. Learn to work a computer or plant a herb garden.

Eileen retired in Phoenix with her husband. They bought a home in a retirement community. Classes of all kinds were offered in the community center. Eileen noticed a weaving class was being offered. She had fond memories of a handmade loom her aunt gave her as a child. She wove squares that her aunt sewed together for a quilt for her doll. She remembers feeling so proud of her work.

She decided to learn about weaving. She purchased a loom and soon was making presents of scarves and tea towels for family and friends. Her hobby developed into a small successful business as her talent became known. Eileen enjoyed herself and felt balanced with accomplishment.

Social balancing can be fun. Let go of ego restrictions and bring out the child in you to balance your psyche. Play. Have fun. Ride those water bumper cars at the fair. Build a snowman or make snow angels after the first snow fall. Run through the sprinklers on a hot summer day. Attend plays that make you laugh. Tell jokes and laugh. Laughter is the sunshine that keeps body and soul in balance.

My friend and I, stressed over family events, decided we needed time out. We took each other out to lunch. On the way home, we stopped at a card shop to buy cards for upcoming family events. We found ourselves reading verses of cards and laughing so much, we attracted attention from other shoppers. They joined us in the fun. Humor is contagious.

SPIRITUAL BALANCE

Spiritual balance brings serenity and inner peace. Making time for connecting with God keeps the mobile of body and soul in harmony. Because body and soul are woven together, spiritual balance elevates our self-esteem. When we "let go" and "let grow" into a spiritual dimension, self-esteem soars.

Spiritual balance does not just happen. Planning and making time for connecting are necessary. Quiet time should be set aside for meditating and communicating with God. We need to reflect on life and the spiritual values we have formed to assess our beliefs. Relaxing physically opens us to meditation. Meditation is mental prayer. It is wordless communication that can lead to the highest form of prayer, contemplation. In contemplation, we simply bask in Divine Love. When we meditate, we reflect on a particular truth, perhaps some event from the life of Christ. Reading the scriptures helps us reflect on spiritual life. We obtain knowledge that helps us grow in love and the desire to bond with our suprapersonal relationships. Meditation prepares us for worship and prayers of petition.

In Matthew 6:9-13, Jesus taught us how to pray:

> *Our Father who art in heaven, hallowed be Thy name;*
> *Thy kingdom come;*
> *Thy will be done on earth as it is in heaven.*
> *Give us this day our daily bread;*
> *And forgive us our debts as we also forgive our debtors,*
> *And lead us not into temptation, but deliver us from evil.*

This beautiful prayer says it all. It combines the dimensions of worship and petition. In communicating these words to our Father, we recognize and revere who God is. We ask to be with him in eternity. We tell him we will live our lives as he has taught us to live them through scriptures. We pray for our physical needs and ask him to forgive us our faults, knowing we must also forgive others for their shortcomings. Finally, we ask God to keep materialism away from us, so we can disconnect from worldly temptations and connect with him.

Every daily act we do has a spiritual meaning. Just living life is spiritual, for life is a mysterious gift. The monk Thomas Merton once wrote, "In modern times, we have lost sight of the fact that even the most ordinary actions of our everyday life are invested, by their very nature, with a deep spiritual meaning."

Going about our work and interacting in our relationships is communicating spiritually. We may not feel emotionally that we are making contact. Bells do not ring to tell us we have been heard, but we need to be persistent. Signs of inner well-being tell us we are connecting.

Take time to gain spiritual knowledge. In my search for a more intimate and personal knowledge of Jesus, I fulfilled a dream of traveling in the Holy Lands. I visited Bethlehem where he was born. I walked where Jesus walked. I bathed in the Sea of Galilee. I waded in the Jordan river. I stood where Jesus preached the Sermon on the Mount. With tears in my eyes, I entered Old Jerusalem and walked the Way of the Cross, the *"Via Dolorosa."* I was like a sponge soaking up all I could to form my intimate relationship with God through his Son. This experience brought the scriptures to life for me. They have new meaning. I have moved from "black and white" understanding to "living color."

We cannot all travel to the Holy Land, but we can avail ourselves of the eucharistic banquet Jesus invites us to share with him. Just as we need food for our physical well-being and growth, so too we need spiritual food for balance. A banquet awaits us at every Mass to nourish our souls.

> *I am the living bread*
> *that has come down from heaven.*
> *If anyone eats of this bread,*
> *he shall live forever;*
> *And the bread that I will give*
> *is my flesh for the life of the world.*
>
> —John 6:51-52

For Reflection

How do you achieve balance in your life?

Physically

- ❧ Do you take care of your body? In what ways?
- ❧ What healthy eating habits do you have?
- ❧ How do you energize yourself?
- ❧ Are you exercising consistently and according to your health?
- ❧ Do you have regular check-ups?

Intellectually

- ❧ Do you stretch your mind with new knowledge?
- ❧ What new hobby or project are you doing?
- ❧ Do you take risks that challenge your lifestyle?
- ❧ List some goals you have set for mind stretching.

Emotionally

- ❧ Do you focus on the present?
- ❧ Are you handling your fears effectively?
- ❧ In what three ways do you diffuse your anger?
- ❧ Give examples of how you love unconditionally.
- ❧ Do you have the patience to wait until you can change something that cannot be changed at present?

Socially

- ❧ Are you able to play just for fun?
- ❧ How do you take care of your child within?
- ❧ Are you working to build better relationships with yourself, others, and God?

Spiritually

❧ Are you taking time to meditate?

❧ How do you transform mediation into prayer?

❧ Do you praise and petition when you talk to God?

❧ Is your faith affected when you think your prayers are not answered?

❧ Think about the senses of sight, hearing, smelling, touching, and tasting. How do you use them to enrich your spiritual life?

PSALM REFLECTION

Read Psalm 136 again.

Praise the Lord of lords;
God's love endures forever;
Who skillfully made the heavens,
God's love endures forever;
Who spread the earth upon the waters,
God's love endures forever;
Who made the great lights,
God's love endures forever;
The sun to rule the day,
God's love endures forever;
The moon and stars to rule the night,
God's love endures forever.

—Psalm 136:3-10

How does this psalm reflect balance in your life?

14
Creating a Wellness Portfolio

Most of us are familiar with financial portfolios. Financial portfolios are designed to invest assets to keep up with inflation and to increase the base. In retirement portfolios, a balance is worked out between the assets held in reserve and the need for disposable income as a budget requires.

A "wellness portfolio" is another very important tool that we can create to ensure proper investment in our well-being. As we age, we have to work harder to keep physically and mentally healthy. Body parts begin to wear. Balance is tipped. Like Kimberly's mobile, we too may need help to float and stabilize. When we record our goals and progress, wellness becomes both tangible and workable.

We need a plan that is focused yet flexible to cover unexpected changes that occur in life. Just as a financial portfolio changes in retirement when finances are limited, so too should a health portfolio be flexible as we age.

We have been developing a wellness plan throughout this book. We have discussed feeling comfortable about ourselves and being able to accept ourselves unconditionally for who we are, not what we do. We have explored healthy relationships with ourselves, others, and God. We have discovered how important it is to be free of damaging expectations to achieve balance and to celebrate life. These are definitions of sound mental health that enable us to meet the demands of aging. Now we need to focus on building our own successful individual portfolios to help us move on in life.

GUIDELINES

To design a successful portfolio, we need guidelines to help us get where we want to go. The following are some general guidelines that I have found helpful:

1. *Focus your energy.* Before we set goals, we need to become focused. When we are focused, we are pursuing life with full attention. We live in the present with awareness of what is happening around us. We open ourselves for opportunities to help us grow.

2. *Set goals.* Establish both long-term and short-term goals. These will help us live each day to its fullest. We need to know the direction we are moving and why.

3. *Be realistic.* A goal needs to be realistic to be reached. It can have some risk compatible with your ability for risk-taking. But if it is unreachable, frustration will only foster a poor self-image. An example of an incompatible goal might be striving to become an opera singer if you do not have such a talent. This goal would be set for failure. But if you love opera, setting a goal to study operas and the artists involved would be reachable and enjoyable.

4. *Challenge yourself.* On the other hand, goals need to be challenging. If they are not challenging, there will be no stretching into growth. The difficult part is knowing the difference between reachable and unreachable. A goal needs to fit into the bigger picture of life. Does it all fit together?

5. *Set priorities.* Concentrating on activities that we feel will be successful will help us refine our choices so that we select the best path for growth possible. By prioritizing our needs and wants, we focus on the most important, making success more attainable. It is a mistake to work on too many goals at the same time.

6. *Be flexible.* Success can only be achieved if we are flexible. Continually evaluating our decision-making helps us to become flexible. Our course of action needs to change when necessary; changes will occur as goals are set in motion.

7. *Get input.* Living our wellness plan entails reacting to opportunities and enlisting the help we need to do so. Brainstorming with others surfaces untapped ideas and hidden talents. Seldom can we accomplish success on our own.

8. *Do your homework.* Studying all aspects of the goal, listing pros and cons, provides a stepping stone for formulating a successful goal. Without knowledge, it is difficult to forecast success.

9. *Plan for change.* A goal is the end toward which effort is directed. A successfully connected goal requires time and hard work. It requires concentration, thinking, and brainstorming before implementing. Before you set goals for your portfolio, reflect on the tension of formulating goals that are not only attainable, but also effective. Effective goals result in significant changes in our lives. They are not created just for the sake of reaching the goal, but to bring about real change. Without change there will be no growth.

10. *Be confident.* Confidence comes from feeling good about ourselves. If we have confidence, we can accomplish what we set out to do. Our goals should not intimidate us. When we set goals that are unreachable or unplanned, we set ourselves up for failure. Our confidence is weakened. We may not have outside encouragement

and need to look inward for support. Confidence is the foundation for inner support.

11. *Hang in there.* We will achieve our goals if we persevere. Setbacks will occur. Progress usually takes the path of two steps forward and one step back. If our expectations focus on this, it will be easier to overcome setbacks. Goals are not instantly obtainable; they evolve. We need to journey from the known to the unknown, re-creating ourselves from facts, hopes, risks, and opportunities that make up our life.

GETTING STARTED

To begin your portfolio, purchase a ringed binder and divider sections. Plan what areas of self you want to improve. Imagine your life as a gigantic puzzle. Which pieces are missing? What goals are needed to complete the picture? Your dividers might be labeled: body wellness, mind challenges, self-esteem, strengthening relationships, and soul-nurturing. Another way to classify areas might be: physical, intellectual, emotional, social, and spiritual. Be creative in designing the structure of your portfolio.

How do you know where to start? Pick a section of your portfolio and begin by brainstorming. Brainstorming is a process where all ideas about a topic are explored. Write down as many ideas as you can think of about the topic you want to work on first. Then prioritize these ideas, labeling the most important number one. It may help to process your ideas with others to get a more accurate base in reality. Now you are ready to form a goal.

I usually put my ideas in diagram form. I make a circle in the middle of a large piece of paper and write in the main theme. For example, physical health. Then I radiate spokes out to other circles that include my brainstorming ideas. This helps me to visualize the goals I could develop to achieve my physical well-being. One spoke can lead to other spokes. The more I fill the page, the more creative I become. When I feel I am drained of ideas, I begin the process of prioritizing, looking for a starting point. I probably would want to check with my doctor for her suggestions on my health needs to see if they match with mine. Now I'm ready to develop my long-term goal and the short-term steps needed to take to climb to success.

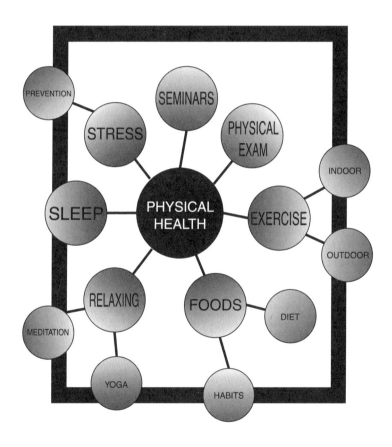

Mary Ann decided her first priority was physical health. She was concerned about osteoporosis. Her bone density scan revealed a rate of bone loss that was alarming. Since she was not taking estrogen because of its side effects, she wanted to be sure her diet was calcium rich and that she was doing bone-strengthening exercise. She did her homework by reading the latest research on osteoporosis and decided to begin with exercise. After discussing the results with her doctor, family, and friends, Mary Ann decided that walking would be the best exercise for her to strengthen her bones.

MAKING A GRID

I have found that the practice of making a grid is a good visual aid to put me on the path toward achieving my goals. Mary Ann displayed her goals on a grid for easy access and tracking.

Walking for Fitness			
	Myself	Alongside Others	With Others
Preparing	Reading Research	Physical exam Walking seminar	Brainstorming
Implementing	Monitor heartbeat	Walk with friend	Walk-a-thon

This grid maps out Mary Ann's long-term goal of walking for fitness, listing short-term goals that would help her reach her destination. She divided her goals into the steps of preparing and implementing. She also organized them into activities she could do individually, those she could do alongside others, and those that would be fulfilled by collaborating with others. Do you recognize these areas as the areas of social development we discussed earlier? Even though these areas of development begin in early play, we continue to grow through these stages.

It also is important to set time limits for accomplishing goals. There needs to be a beginning and end. Mary Ann wrote time increments under her grid that she felt would be comfortable for her. She wanted to accomplish her main goal in three months. However, she realized she needed to be flexible to account for the interruptions in her life. She was ready to expand the time limit to five months, but no longer.

She developed her time plan as follows:

1. Preparation: reading, physical exam, attending a seminar and brainstorming—one month.

2. Implementation: monitoring her heartbeat for a target zone while walking—one week; building up to a 45-minute brisk walk daily with a friend—two months.

3. Walking for breast cancer research—five months.

Mary Ann reached her goal in six months. She felt energized physically and esteemed emotionally.

Judy began her portfolio by preparing a grid in the area of Mind Challenges. Judy was finding herself becoming forgetful. This worried her, especially since her father died of Alzheimer's disease. She wanted to stretch her mind to keep intellectually alert.

Judy was always interested in writing. She had kept a journal for years, but never had the time or the motivation to write a book. Now that her children were grown and on their own, the yearning returned. Her dream was to be a mystery writer. She especially was interested in English mysteries. She devoured books written by authors such as P.D. James, Martha Grimes, and Josephine Tey. She decided to tackle her dream. She set her long-term goal and unfolded short-term goals that would bring her success.

Write a Mystery Novel for Publication			
	Myself	Alongside Others	With Others
Preparing	Research that genre	Attend a writing seminar	Brainstorm
Implementing	Write outline	Send query letters	Complete the manuscript with an editor

Judy set time limits for her goals. Two months for preparing, research, attending a seminar, and brainstorming seemed reasonable. She planned one month for developing an outline and one month for sending out query letters. She planned six months to write the book.

After sending out ten query letters to mystery publishers and receiving negative responses, she was ready to give up her goal. Family and friends encouraged her to persevere. One publisher had suggested she try writing a short story for a mystery magazine. Judy was determined to be published, so she set aside her novel for the time being to write a short story. She amended her grid and proceeded to accomplish her new goal.

Write a Mystery Short Story for Publication			
	Myself	Alongside Others	With Others
Preparing	Read magazines	Attend seminar	Brainstorm plot ideas
Implementing	Develop outline	Query magazines	Complete story with an editor

Once again Judy set her time limits. This time she was successful. Her short story was published in a mystery magazine. Being flexible helped her to realize her goal of being published.

Alyce decided to set her first goal under the section of Soul-Nurturing She wanted to improve her relationship with God. Over the years, she had drifted away from her faith. Now in her later life, religion was becoming important to her. After brainstorming, she determined that meditating was the key to connecting with God. Her goal was to improve her inner reflection. She designed a grid to accomplish her goal.

Improve My Reflective Prayer		
	Myself	Alongside Others	With Others
Preparing	Read scriptures	Research meditation methods	Join a yoga class
Implementing	15-minute daily contempation	Communicate with God through prayer	Attend a retreat

As Alyce worked on her goals and improved at meditation, she began to feel closer to God. She set her time for preparation for one month, implementation for two months. Alyce found that it became easier to meditate as she set aside time and practiced. She found that worship and prayers of petition flowed naturally as she connected with God.

EVALUATING YOUR PROGRESS

Once you begin to work on your goals, it is important to evaluate your progress. Sizing up where you are on the grid declares how much has been accomplished and what still needs to be done. Evaluating produces feedback. If your short term goals are not leading to your main goal, feedback will help you change direction before too much effort has been involved.

An evaluation can be as simple as summarizing in a few sentences or answering questions on a form. You may want to use the evaluation form that follows or make up one of your own. An evaluation sheet at the end of each section might look like this:

EVALUATING MY GOALS

1. Are my goals reachable?
2. Do I step my short-term goals in small increments to make reaching my main goal easier?
3. Have I set comfortable time limits to accomplish my goals?

4. How has putting my goals into grid form helped me to visualize reaching my objectives?

5. Have I been flexible enough to change my grid if it is not working?

6. Which goals have been successfully reached? Which have not?

7. How can I improve my goals for success?

8. How has my life become more balanced by keeping a Wellness Portfolio?

In summary, develop one specific goal at a time. Prioritize your needs and develop your goals accordingly. Develop your long-term goal with short-term goals on a grid for easy viewing and implementing. Be sure you set time limits for each goal so you see a beginning and an end. Write them down under your grid. Be flexible. You may have to adjust goals or time limits, as life happenings may interfere. From time to time, evaluate your progress. Keep your progress reports at the end of each section to add to or review.

Keeping a portfolio helps us keep track of how we are balancing our life. As we age, we become resistant to growth because growth means change, and change makes us uncomfortable. We need to rethink our mortality so we can keep growing. Life, after all, is a stepping stone to another stage of living—eternity. We have all been given talents and abilities that sometimes lie dormant inside of us. While they are varied, we all are equal in God's eyes. No one of us is greater or lesser than the other, only different. We need to make our own way through life to eternity, and that takes planning and commitment.

PSALM REFLECTION

How varied are your works, Lord!
In wisdom you have wrought them all:
the earth is full of your creatures.
May the glory of the Lord endure forever;

may the Lord be glad in these works!
I will sing to the Lord all my life:
I will sing praise to my God while I live.
May my theme be pleasing to God;
I will rejoice in the Lord.

    —Psalm 104:24, 31,33, 34

Read all of Psalm 104. In this psalm, God easily and skill-fully creates a world vibrant with life. Compare your creation of self with God's creation of the world.

❧ Are you creating yourself to be fully alive?

❧ How is the Lord present in your "work" of creation?

❧ Explain how freedom is interwoven with creation.

❧ Is your theme pleasing to God? In what way?

Part IV

Soul-Nurturing

15
Discovering Your Inner Beauty

Mary looked at her reflection in the mirror. Could this really be her? Where was that creamy, smooth, flawless complexion, those pink cheeks and the clear eyes that sparkled? Inside she saw herself as a young woman, but this was the face of a 60-year-old.

A snore filled the quiet room. Mary turned and looked at Jim sleeping soundly in bed. Where was that handsome, strong, young man she fell in love with? Aging was something that happened to someone else, not to her. Aging is a sickness, she thought as her eyes filled with tears.

Senior years can be a dead end to life. They can be filled with frustration, bitterness, anger, and remorse. But they don't have to be that way. Aging is but another stage, a doorway rather than a dead end. The gift of life that God has given us is more than physical. We have a spiritual part of us, a soul, that lives on. But like the other dimensions of our lives, this part also requires nurturing, commitment, and planning, if it is to grow into eternity. The poet Robert Browning expressed it beautifully:

Grow old along with me!
The best is yet to be,
The last of life, for which the first was made:
Our times are in his hand
Who saith, "A whole I planned,
Youth shows but half, trust God:
See all, nor be afraid!"

Our soul is cemented to our physical body as we move through life. It needs to be probed, cared for, stimulated, and nurtured just as we tend to our physical body. We need to give it roots and wings, roots in our being and wings to fly home.

How do we identify our soul? How does our soul show itself? Our soul is that very deepest part of us. The part that mingles happiness with sadness. When we are touched so deeply by beauty that our joy turns to tears, it is our soul that is being stirred. Artists have the talent to touch our souls. A beautiful painting, a sacred piece of music, or a glorious sunset painted by God awakens our souls.

When I was a little girl, I experienced two parts to me. When I would lean over the arm of our couch, my stomach would feel so strange. I wondered at the deep sensation. Was this my soul? I wondered why I was in my body and not inside someone else's? Somehow I felt there was something deep inside of me that was not my physical body. It's this part of me that I tried to touch.

Whenever I hear Schubert's *Ave Maria*, my soul is touched. The music expresses my innermost feelings and brings such joy that tears come to my eyes. My soul is nourished with my deepest feelings of beauty.

Exercise
Think back to an occasion when you were deeply moved.

❦ What was the occasion?

❦ Who or what was involved?

❦ What feelings did you experience?

❦ Describe what this meant to you.

❦ Could you feel a deeper part of you being touched?

When Mary looked in the mirror, she became depressed. She could see only her outer self. Beauty depended on the appearance of her physical body, which was aging. Beauty became an end in itself, and this led to a sense of hopelessness. This was fertile ground for depression. Her inner beauty was hidden; she had forgotten the light in her soul.

Feelings and emotions, intense feelings, are gateways that lead us to the light of our inner beauty. They make us fully human. They connect with our soul. For effective soul connecting we need to handle feelings and emotions in ways that do not interfere with our daily life, our relationships, and our work. It is amazing how many feelings we are able to experience.

Some "up" feelings include: accepted, affectionate, amused, calm, confident, contented, curious, determined, elated, enthusiastic, interested, friendly, grateful, happy, loving, mischievous, optimistic, pleased, proud, relieved, satisfied, thrilled, trusting, and worthy.

Some "down" feelings include: abandoned, afraid, anxious, apprehensive, ashamed, belittled, crushed, defeated, depressed, disappointed, discouraged, fearful, frightened, frustrated, guilty, helpless, humiliated, hurt, insecure, lonely, misunderstood, neglected, pessimistic, rejected, sad, unloved, and worthless.

Some "angry" feelings include: aggressive, annoyed, belligerent, bitter, disgusted, enraged, envious, furious, inflamed, irritated, mean, negative, obstinate, paranoid, pressured, resentful, surly, threatened, and vindictive.

Some "confused" feelings include: amazed, astonished, conflicted, disoriented, nervous, perplexed, puzzled, shocked, startled, surprised, tense, uncertain, undecided, and uneasy.

Some "detached" feelings include: aloof, apathetic, bored, empty, indifferent, listless, lukewarm, numb, sluggish, unconcerned, uninterested, and vacant.

Feelings are not positive or negative. They just are. They are part of the total us. They make us human. We are not accountable for experiencing feelings. What we are responsible for is how we act out our feelings. These actions are either acceptable or unacceptable behavior.

We do not all experience feelings with the same intensity. Certain emotions may flare up brightly in some or just glow in others. Our temperaments, part of our genetic make up, determine our capacity to experience and cope with feelings. This is why Sarah has difficulty coping with her intense feelings of anger while Helen is able to control her less intense anger easily. Of course environmental factors enter the picture as well. How we are taught to handle feelings and emotions through parenting and the modeling of others helps determine our reactions to what we feel.

Keep in mind that feelings can be mixed together and may be difficult to unravel. Anger, for example, is an umbrella feeling. It covers other feelings that need probing to surface. Unless these other feelings are identified, the anger will fester and remain out of our control. When a feeling interferes with our quality of life, we have lost control.

Feelings denied do not go away. Unhealthy attitudes about expressing feelings surround us. One such attitude describes humility as repression of feelings. To become humble means to strip away layers to our inner core. It means letting go of false pride, arrogance, aggression, and selfishness. Humility does not occur by ignoring or suppressing feelings. In order to become humble we need to touch, recognize, and express our feelings assertively without intrusion on others or harm to self. Jesus exemplified this humility. He expressed feelings of love, concern, empathy, and even anger.

And they came to Jerusalem. And he entered the temple, and began to cast out those who were selling and buying in the temple; and he overturned the tables of the money-changers and the seats of those who sold the doves. He would not allow anyone to carry a vessel through the temple. And he began to teach, saying to them, "Is it not written, 'My house shall be called a house of prayer for all nations'? But you have made it a den of thieves" (Mk 12:15-17).

We know that feelings and emotions are linked with our entire biological system. They are woven together intimately. They affect our self-image, our behavior, our interactions with others, and our relationship with God.

Every time you experience an intense emotion your body prepares for defense. Your heart beats faster. Digestion slows down. Blood rushes to outer limbs. There is a stimulation of the liver and sweat glands. Pupils of the eyes dilate to let in more vision. Coagulation of the blood is increased.

When feelings are repressed, pressure builds and erupts somewhere in our body. Headaches, breathing difficulties, stomach problems, intestinal spasms, and high blood pressure may be attributed to improper expressions of feelings.

Exercise

Keep a daily journal. It is a good way to keep in touch with your feelings. It is important to become aware of your emotional strengths and weaknesses. Summarize your day by recalling significant incidents and the emotions you experienced.

- ❦ How did you handle them?
- ❦ Was your mind in control or did your feelings run away with you?
- ❦ How did you resolve the situation?

❦ Are you experiencing guilt feelings?

❦ What could you have done to better the situation?

PSALM REFLECTION

Ponder these words:

> *Lord, you have probed me, you know me:*
> *you know when I sit and stand;*
> *you understand my thoughts from afar.*
> *My travels and my rest you mark;*
> *with all my ways you are familiar.*
> *Even before a word is on my tongue,*
> *Lord, you know it all.*
> *Behind and before you encircle me*
> *and rest your hand upon me.*
> *Such knowledge is beyond me,*
> *far too lofty for me to reach.*
> *Probe me, God, know my heart;*
> *try me, know my concerns.*
> *See if my way is crooked,*
> *then lead me in the ancient paths.*

> —Psalm 139:1-6, 23-24

❦ "Lord, you have probed me, you know me." Help me to know myself.

❦ "You know when I sit and stand." Help me to understand how my responses to my feelings affect my self-image, my relationships with others and with you.

❦ "You understand my thoughts from afar." Help me to explore the innermost thoughts and feelings that touch my soul.

16
Emotions: Touching the Soul

Emotional balance is a connection to our deepest self. Handling feelings and emotions in healthy ways that do not interfere with daily living opens windows to our souls. When we are in touch with our emotions, stable and centered, we are in touch with our soul.

When basic needs are satisfied, when we feel loved and esteemed, it is easier to be in control of our feelings. We are able to express our feelings in non-aggressive ways. As we age, we may feel that our basic needs are being threatened or sabotaged. Our feelings come to our defense, sometimes becoming uncontrolled. When we lose the ability to be in touch with our feelings and have no sense of perspective on them, it's as if the window to our soul has closed.

Cynthia was looking forward to her husband's retirement. She envisioned time to travel, time to be together, and time to spend with children and grandchildren. The retirement party was a wonderful send-off for her husband. Cynthia never realized what a valued employee he was. Two months later they were ready to embark on a long-anticipated trip. They had gone to bed early the night before. In the morning Cynthia quickly got up, showered, and was surprised to see her husband still in bed. She went to wake him and found he was dead.

The shock of his death was overwhelming. Her security was shattered. After weeks of denial, she became intensely angry. At first she directed her anger toward her husband. Why didn't he take better care of himself? Then she directed her anger toward God. How could a loving God do this to her? She gave up her faith and became jealous of any happiness her family and friends experienced, forcing them to retreat. This angered her all the more. Her anger was out of control. It ruled her life.

We all need to feel loved and esteemed. We need to feel accepted by others. When we lose others through relocation, illness, or death, our needs become threatened, and our feelings are more difficult to manage. We do not feel secure as change affects our lives. As our health becomes more frail, our independence weakens. The moral standards we have set for ourselves— kindness, courage, honesty, generosity, and justice—seem to be of no avail. This is the time in our lives that we need to surround ourselves with people who can reinforce our strengths, not our weaknesses, who will not enable us to continue allowing our feelings to control us.

We need to take responsibility for our reactions to our feelings. We have become experts at defending ourselves against this concept. Sayings such as: "You hurt my feelings," "You make me angry," "You are embarrassing me," and "I can't help feeling the way I do," make others responsible for our feelings. Our feelings come from our response to our life situations. How we react to these situations is our responsibility alone. Let's explore some troublesome feelings which, when not dealt with, can cut us off from our soul.

ANGER

Anger is one feeling that we do not know what to do with. Because anger is usually directed toward someone, we later feel guilt or remorse. Intelligent solutions to concerns are difficult to achieve when the anger gets in the way. We need to become aware of some of the properties of this intense emotion.

Anger covers up other feelings. Perhaps it is disappointment in someone we trusted. We may have been hurt by someone close to us. Anger becomes our defense. We may be jealous of a friend who is young looking or envious of our children who have more material things than we had at their age.

We tend to displace anger. It is easier to blame others than to accept responsibility for our feeling. We act passive-aggressively. Instead of directing our anger to the source of our problem, we direct it to the nearest person. Our anger is not resolved and we have triggered uneasiness in another.

Anger signifies loss of control. We need to ask ourselves, "What do I feel helpless about?" I remember substitute-teaching in a school that promoted paddling to discipline children. I was assigned to the fourth grade. In the teachers' lounge, the teachers were discussing how not to lose control of their class. "Thank goodness for the paddle," one teacher exclaimed. They didn't realize that in using the paddle they had already lost control. Even more importantly, they were teaching children to solve their problems by hitting. I did not teach in that school again as the principal was unbending on this issue.

Knowing that it is not socially acceptable to hurt ourselves, hurt others, or destroy property, we need proper outlets for our anger. It is important to plan ahead before feelings erupt. Decide on two or three specific ways to diffuse your anger. Set aside a pillow to punch. Write in a journal. Once you see your feeling expressed on paper, it is easier to deal with. Do some baking. Kneading bread is a wonderful and safe way to release anger. Run cool water over your wrists. Water is soothing and relaxing. Select from other ways that are acceptable to you. What is important is that you follow through with something. Once anger is expressed in safe ways and under control, decisions can be made rationally.

Ask yourself if your anger is useful. Anger can touch our soul in constructive ways. If it helps us to set new goals to move on in life it can be beneficial.

Susan was in a dead end job. She disliked her work. She typed on a computer all day. She was a people-person and was happiest interacting with others. Susan felt she could not take the risk of changing jobs. At work one morning, she found a memo on her desk stating that the report she had spent hours completing was to be set aside as the company decided to go another direction. She was very upset and brought her anger home. She hurt those she loved and realized something had to change. This crisis motivated Susan to search for a new job. Today Susan is happy and fulfilled as a receptionist in a doctor's office. Anger helped Susan to move on in her life. Her self-image improved. Her soul was touched.

DEPRESSION

Depression is the most common complaint of older adults. Seniors have experienced many losses through the years. They often deal with grieving. Most of my clients come to counseling with symptoms of depression. As a therapist, my first strategy is to validate their feelings, giving them permission to feel depression without guilt.

Three types of depression surface. Occasional depression is what we all feel now and then. It may or may not be related to a specific loss. It may last a few hours or a few days. Acute depression is a normal reaction to a specific loss. Usually it does not affect self-image once grief is processed through stages. Chronic depression occurs over a long period of time and becomes part of the personality. The person feels useless. Life has no meaning. Contact is lost with others. It becomes an illness. When a person is clinically depressed, one thing that may happen is that levels of serotonin, a chemical found in the brain, may drop. If this happens, medication along with counseling may be needed.

Signs of depression may include: feeling unusually sad or irritable, having trouble sleeping, finding it difficult to concentrate, losing appetite, lacking energy, and losing pleasure in living. Procrastination and perfectionism may indicate depression. Depression may be triggered by a crisis such as divorce, relocation, retirement, illness, aging, or the death of a loved one. It can also come on for no apparent reason. The intensity and duration of the feeling determines the treatment.

Depression touches our soul. It reaches the deepest part of us. It is a way our body copes with trauma. It is a turning inward for healing, reflection, and regrouping. When we are shocked, all systems close down in defense. Body and soul work together for healing. Jesus was in the depths of depression and despair as he hung on the cross. His body and soul cried out together for healing: "My God, my God, why have you forsaken me?" (Mt 27:46). And then as healing occurred, he cried out in a loud voice, "Father into your hands I commend my spirit" (Lk 23:46).

When you feel depressed, use your mind. Ask yourself what has happened or what is going on in your life that has triggered this feeling. Most of us are aware of the feeling, but not the thoughts behind the feeling. When you encounter a crisis, pay attention to what your self-talk is telling you. When we feel depressed, we use our negative thoughts to perpetuate the depression. We tell ourselves how worthless we are, that nobody likes us, all this is my fault, or no one else could have the problems we do. We need to change our negative thoughts to positive ones.

Kathy felt her life was going nowhere. Her family lived far from her. Phone calls became fewer and fewer as her children became more and more involved with their own families. She found herself in bed longer. Some days she did not even bother to dress. She stopped going to church or calling friends. Her negative thoughts took over. "No one likes me. They do not want to be around me. I can't do anything right." Kathy's negative thoughts became her self-talk.

Changing self-talk is not easy. Negative thoughts need to be replaced with positive ones. "Some people may not like me, but I know some who do." "My children want to be here, but family obligations and work prevent it." "I make mistakes, but I can learn from them." Counseling may be needed to help you to change your self-talk.

Depression is contagious. Try to be around happy people. It is important that you do activities even when you do not feel like it. I usually have my clients make a simple daily schedule for themselves. For example: get out of bed at 8:00 A.M., shower, have breakfast, plan and implement an outing, or call a friend. Cook something for dinner, watch TV or read, prepare for bed. Sometimes the depression is so severe, only basic needs can be met. What is important is that there is movement and that you get the help you need.

GUILT AND WORRY

Guilt and worry are two common feelings that prevent us from living in the present. Guilt is about past behavior, while worry is trying to control behavior of the future. Both prevent us from moving on in life. They immobilize us. As we age, our memories become more important to us. In remembering others, we experience guilt over what we did not do. As we become more vulnerable with age, we worry more about what the future holds for us, fearing our loss of independence. Unless we can do something about these feelings, they take up our precious time and do not nourish our souls.

Guilt can be rooted in childhood memories. It can also be self-inflicted, usually from values we have set for ourselves that may or may not be realistic. Guilt based in childhood experiences usually originates from trying to please others, particularly a parent or other authority figure. The following are examples of admonitions that may have triggered guilt feelings as a child:

"Mommy won't like it if you won't eat your potatoes."

"Wait until your father comes home!"

"Shame on you!"

These types of statements carry over into adulthood. We hear their echoes in these statements:

"How can you go fishing and leave me all alone?"

"You didn't empty the garbage. Now my back is hurting again because I had to do your job."

"How could you say that to me? I'm your mother and I'm old. You won't have me around much longer."

Guilt can also be self-inflicted. The values that we have formed by mirroring others, in formal education, and in all of our experiences determine our belief systems. When we violate these beliefs, we experience guilt. These belief systems may not be realistic, causing us to experience conflict between the value we have formed and reality. As we have seen before, statements such as, "If only I had . . ." "I should (shouldn't) have . . ." signal self-inflicted guilt.

Grace's faith was rooted in the lessons she learned in childhood from the Baltimore Catechism. Her self-talk based on her belief system sent the message that it was a mortal sin to miss Sunday Mass unless she was gravely ill. This Sunday a close friend asked her to spend the day at the coast. They were to leave early in the morning. This meant she would have to miss Mass. Grace did not drive and wanted to go, as she did not get out often. She made the decision to go with her friend. That night she was riddled with guilt. She shouldn't have gone. God would never forgive her. She knew she had committed a mortal sin. She could repeat word for word what the Baltimore Catechism defined as mortal sin.

To make a sin mortal these three things are necessary: first, the thought, desire, word, action, or omission must be seriously wrong or considered seriously wrong; second, the sinner must know it is seriously wrong; third, the sinner must fully consent to it.

Grace's scrupulous conscience sent the message loud and clear. "You have committed a mortal sin." She called her parish priest and asked to go to confession as soon as possible. She needed to rid herself of guilt.

We need to be able to look at interactions and take responsibility for those under our control and not take responsibility for those situations out of our control.

Exercise

Answer the following questions. They may help you tap into your guilt feelings.

❦ What do I feel most guilty about at this time in my life?

❦ What has triggered this feeling in me?

❦ What part am I responsible for?

❦ Is there anything I can do to show my responsibility?

❦ Is there something reinforcing my guilt feelings and causing me to hang on to them? What is it?

❦ Can I own my guilt, forgive myself, and move on?

Worry involves the future. It is mental distress or anxiety resulting from concern, usually over something impending or anticipated that we have no assurance of happening. Worry is not the same as planning for the future. One is productive, one is not. When we set goals for our future, we are growing. When we worry, we stop growing. We become immobilized. As we age, our concerns can spill over into worry instead of action. We worry about our families, our health, our mortality, and money to pay bills. The list is endless. Ridding ourselves of worry is difficult. If you find yourself worrying excessively, try some of these suggestions.

Exercise

Develop a plan of action for your worry. Guilt and worry can be soul touching if we can take responsibility for our feelings and bring them into the here and now for healthy action.

❦ Try to identify what will change by your worry.

❦ Set aside ten minutes each day as worry time. Then worry.

❦ Keep a running list of worries. Prioritize them. Pick only the top one to worry about.

Pray:

> *Probe me, God, know my heart;*
> *try me, know my concerns.*
> *See if my way is crooked,*
> *then lead me in the ancient paths.*

—Psalm 139:23-24

FEAR AND ANXIETY

Fear and anxiety walk hand in hand. When we are fearful, we become anxious. Fear touches our souls when it moves us into action to better our lives. Our fears as we grow older differ from fears we may have had as a child. As seniors we fear outcomes of health problems. We fear insecurity. We fear dependency. We fear loneliness. We fear our own mortality or losing those we love. Our fears are based on not knowing outcomes rather than the "things" we may have been afraid of as children.

Sometimes we carry over fears from our childhood: fear of dogs, fear of the dark, fear of snakes or spiders, fear of water. No matter how silly they may seem, fears are very real to us. So real that they may cause anxiety or panic attacks. When fears are out of control and take over our lives, it's time for professional help.

Evelyn came into counseling because she was having panic attacks. They would occur "out of the blue." She would feel light-headed, and it became difficult for her to breath. Her heartbeat accelerated, and she experienced chest pain that brought her into the emergency room. The symptoms would disappear after awhile. She was able to go on with her day, but fear clung to her, as she did not know when the panic attacks would return.

As we worked in counseling, she identified her crippling fear. She feared that her husband Bob would leave her. He had an affair five years ago, and although she told herself she had worked through all this and forgiven him, she felt it was only a matter of time before it would happen again. Her fear had festered for five years. She was afraid to talk to him about her concerns, thinking this would upset him. The panic attacks had been occurring for about a year and were becoming increasingly worse.

I suggested both husband and wife come in for marriage counseling. As we worked together, it became evident she was strangling him with lack of trust, and he was putting demands on her appearance as an excuse for the absence of intimacy. As I helped Evelyn grow in independence and helped Bob to take responsibility for his actions, Evelyn's panic attacks subsided.

Intense fears become phobias. As we become phobic, we are motivated toward unpleasant situations determined by the reality we create rather than what really is. Phobias can be cured. In counseling we try to help the person become aware of the fear and move toward a realistic reaction to the fear. Some ways to cope with your fears include:

Try to identify the fear.

Recognize and give yourself permission to feel the fear. Nothing will happen to you.

Take some deep breaths and think pleasant thoughts.

Make your self-talk logical. "I'm OK. I won't die. Calm down."

Study all you can about the thing you fear and how to defend yourself. The more you know about what you fear, the less frightening it becomes.

Try to formulate a plan of action to make the fear manageable, to bring it under your control.

Find ways to stay independent. Dependency increases fear.

Once you've gained control of a fear, allow it to touch your soul in a climate of mystery rather than danger.

Seek professional help if you are not getting results.

To allow feelings to touch our souls, we need to experience troublesome feelings in ways that decrease the pain and increase a sense of wellness. As these feelings connect with our souls, we will be able to turn them into creativity. As with all pain, some good prevails.

Exercise

Try this exercise to keep in touch with your feelings. Take a large piece of paper and some crayons. Get comfortable at a table or on the floor. Think about a feeling you are having trouble with.

- ❦ What incident happened that triggered that feeling?
- ❦ Where did it happen?
- ❦ Who was involved?
- ❦ Close your eyes. Feel the feeling. What parts of your body are affected?

Now try to put that feeling on paper. You may use colors or lines or circles to express your emotion. Sometimes more than one feeling may be on your paper, as feelings are difficult to separate. If you are working on anger, fear may seep through. That's OK. It may help you get in touch with what is really going on.

REFLECTION

Jesus used his anger to make God's temple a holy place. He turned his depression and pain on the cross to love as he saved us all. He turned his fear of death to courage as an example for us. He turned distressful feelings into healing feelings.

- ❦ Think about a painful feeling you have experienced.
- ❦ Were you able to turn it around?
- ❦ How did you do this?
- ❦ What good came from this feeling? Explain.

17
Values: Developing the Soul

We do not hear much about values today. This is disheartening to those of us who were raised on values such as honor, trust, responsibility, courage, loyalty, truth, justice, and charity. Unfortunately, society has decided it is more important to concentrate on the values of power and materialism, achieving financial success no matter what the cost—"Me-ness" instead of "You-ness." These latter values do not open the soul to growth. The soul is ignored. The deepest part of us begins to wither. Our life becomes shallow without direction to eternity.

Values are those things that we cherish most. A value is a principle or quality of intrinsic importance. It is what we prize or esteem. Values form our belief systems. Our belief systems have taken years to formulate. They form our self-talk and lead us to action.

Belief systems built from values affect many areas of living. We formulate opinions about religion, politics, family, friends, money, crime, sex, health, work, and death. We make decisions daily based on our values. Sometimes our values are not clear, and we are confused about what to do. Our world offers us many choices. Which are best for us as mature women? Our values change as we age. What once was important to us may not be at this time in our life. Concerns we experience now are not the same as in our youth.

Janice remembers that when she was about eight or nine, fairness was of extreme importance. She remembers arguing that her brother was getting more marshmallows in his cereal than she was. A very wise mother had her count out each tiny piece of marshmallow to be sure all was fair. She began to count, and then, realizing how impractical this was, gave up, allowing her mother to make the judgment. Janice began the process of formulating a value. This value of fairness eventually led to her the tenet of her belief system that life is not always fair.

Processing values involves several steps. We must be able to choose among alternatives. This means exploring the options available, gaining the knowledge necessary to make a good decision. We need to examine how this value will affect our lives. We should reflect on how the values we choose will influence our belief systems.

Consequences need to be considered. If I choose this value, what consequences will occur? Am I responsible enough to accept these consequences? Perhaps friends may turn away from me. Am I prepared to accept this?

The choice must be freely made. Is someone pressuring you to make this decision? The pressure may be subtle and not recognized. It can be a simple statement from a person close to you, such as, "Oh, you always were so right and proper." The pressure resulting from such statements can be very strong.

For a value to be authentic, it must be lived. There must be a repeated pattern of action; it must become part of your life. Sometimes we give lip service to a value, but when circumstances arise, we back down.

Iris believed abortion was murder. She worked long hours in a pro-life counseling center where young pregnant girls were advised to deliver their babies. She worked on an adoption committee to find homes for the newborn babies. When her granddaughter became pregnant at fifteen, Iris was shocked. She could not accept this crisis so close to home. She counseled her granddaughter to have an abortion. Iris' belief system was shaken as her value of being pro-life did not fit the demands of living the value.

Values should not only be cherished, but upheld and declared when appropriate. The apostle Peter's value of loyalty was tested. He chose denial as Jesus foretold:

> Now Simon Peter was standing there keeping warm. And they said to him, "You are not one of his disciples, are you?" He denied it and said, "I am not." One of the slaves of the high priest, a relative of the one whose ear Peter had cut off, said, "Didn't I see you in the garden with him?" Again Peter denied it. And the cock crowed (Jn 18:25-27).

"Values are caught." This expression has been around a long time. We catch values from others covertly. Modeling values provides mirrors for others. As very young children, we wanted to please our parents. We mirrored their actions, not understanding the meaning behind them. At nine or ten years of age we began to develop our reasoning ability. We could begin to understand some intentions behind the actions. At this age, we moved outside the home for role models. We watched our heros' actions and wanted to imitate them. We modeled their values. If we were fortunate to pick models of integrity, our values began to form in this direction. Values are also taught. We learn values. Can you remember values that were taught overtly in your home while you were growing up?

Darlene was brought up in a traditional family. Her father went to work and brought home the money. Nothing more was expected of him. Mother raised the children and kept house. This was all that Darlene wanted of her marriage. When her husband lost his job, money became tight, and living expenses were not being met. He suggested Darlene look for work to help out with expenses. This was against the belief system formulated from the value she learned in her home. The value was expressed in this manner: "There is something wrong with a man who cannot financially support his family." The stress in their relationship brought them into counseling.

Values differ among individuals, families, neighbor-hoods, cities, and countries. Family members live apart and develop values foreign to us. We live in a time when we may not even know our next-door neighbor. Neighbors that we do know do not see values as we do. We are left with no support for our belief systems.

Perhaps you can remember when values among people seemed much the same. My early childhood was spent in a suburb of Chicago. It was a neighborhood of Italians and Czechs. Neighbors sat on porches after dinner while children played in the streets until the street lights went on. If our parents were inside, our neighbors watched us. If we did something wrong, we were reprimanded by whoever witnessed what we did. Our parents heard about it and continued the reprimand. It was as if we were all one family. Values were the same and were supported by everyone.

Teachers taught from the same set of values as our parents. Much to our dismay, our parents took sides with our teachers. It was easy for us to know right from wrong. If we didn't, we soon learned. Jefferson School graduated students with much the same values. I met my husband in this school. We met in kindergarten, and even though we went our separate ways to high school and college, we found each other again. I'm sure similar values played a role in our decision to make a life-long commitment to each other.

As we age, our values need fine tuning. If they are a little flat, not meaningful in our life, we need to tune them to full tone. If they are a little sharp, they need to be tuned down. They need to fit where we are in life if we are to develop the music of our soul. We need to clarify our values, what is important to us and what is not. What values am I carrying around with me that I no longer need? What new values am I developing that will help nurture my soul?

Exercise

Answer these questions to help clarify what values you are living.

❦ What important decisions are you currently involved in?

❦ What feelings are being triggered?

❦ How is your soul, the deepest part of you, being touched?

❦ Make a list of values that you feel are under consideration in making these decisions.

❦ Are these authentic values? Do they fit the criteria?

❦ If not, what new values are you formulating?

❦ How will these values affect your belief systems?

❦ How will these new values help you in your decision making?

As we enter the autumn of our lives, we feel we have reached moral maturity. What exactly is moral maturity? A definition we might begin with is knowledge of right and wrong and the will to act on this knowledge, sanctioned by our soul. Our values give us the knowledge of what we may or may not do. If we fully believe in our values, then our soul will approve of how we will act. We will feel congruent, put together. Perhaps this is what makes us morally mature.

STAGES OF VALUE DEVELOPMENT

Values may differ among individuals, but the development of adult morality is the same for all of us, according to Lawrence Kohlberg, a developmental psychologist. We progress through defined stages. We move through these stages according to our intellectual growth and influences from our environment. The passages through morality trigger developmental stages of our souls.

In the first stage of development, right and wrong are determined by fear of punishment. Our moral actions are determined by the physical consequences of our behavior. We act because we fear punishment. Those of us who were raised on the *Baltimore Catechism* followed religious practices to avoid the wrath of God. We did not want to spend eternity burning in hell. Yes, we were afraid of God. The Old Testament stories appealed to this level of rational development. It was effective because the teachings could be understood by the people on this moral level.

Donna had left the church a long time ago. She felt God had no place in her life. Donna invited her close friend out to lunch. She offered to drive. While they were driving to the restaurant, a drunk driver crashed into them. Donna was seriously injured and her friend was killed. Donna's family and friends tried to reassure her that what happened was not her fault, all to no avail. Donna was sure God was punishing her for turning away from him and that he would never forgive her. She spent many months in counseling trying to convert her image of God, to move from a fearful God to a forgiving God.

In the second stage of soul development we find ourselves morally expecting something in return for our actions. We decide what is right or wrong by the fairness of how others treat us. If I do something for you, I expect you to do something for me. Behavior consists of satisfying one's own needs, and perhaps someone else will be helped in the process.

Julia was waiting for Carole to call. She certainly was not going to call her. She had called her the last three times. It didn't matter that Carole was suffering with arthritis and needed friends for support. Julia felt the least Carole could do was to call her. It was her turn.

Recognition is more valuable than material reward in stage three of moral development. Being nice and being approved by others motivates those of us on this level of soul maturity. Good behavior is defined as helping someone and being praised by them.

Debbie saw an opportunity to help her church. She was asked to head a fund-raising committee. A fashion show was decided upon. Debbie spent hours making this event happen. It was a success, bringing in more money than any other previous project. When the awards banquet was held, Debbie knew she would be honored. She purposely remembered to recognize each committee member. Someone asked for a round of applause for Debbie, but no plaque or flowers were presented to her. She was crushed. Nobody appreciated her work.

The fourth level of determining what is right or wrong is probably where most people see themselves. They consider it their moral duty to follow laws and rules that have been made by those in authority. The law is rigid and unquestionable. Laws are there for a reason, whether we agree with them or not. Social order is above all else, including the individual.

Susan was upset when she returned home from her doctor's appointment. The doctor had ordered tests for her that were intrusive. She didn't understand why she needed these tests. She was frightened about going through such tests and had questions that she never asked. To Susan, doctors represented an authority you did not question. When she had tried to ask a question, the busy doctor brushed her off and said she had no other choice. Susan accepted this, but felt she was being taken advantage of.

On the fifth level, principles become involved. Right and wrong are defined not only by fixed laws, but by consideration of individual values. Laws agreed upon must take into consideration all of society. Development in this stage of morality considers the individual.

Violet was called for jury duty. The letter she received stated in no uncertain terms what the law was in regard to jury duty. Violet knew the law was necessary to uphold our justice system. However, there had to be exceptions that took into consideration individuals' needs also. She wrote to the county explaining the hardship this would create in her family. She was the only caretaker for her invalid mother who needed twenty-four-hour care. There was no money to provide for her care, and unless the county could provide help, she would have to rescind. Her letter was accepted.

The sixth level of determining right and wrong is the highest level of development. Very few of us reach this level because it requires great sacrifice. It reaches the very depth of our souls. Right and wrong are based on abstract and ethical principles. Specific laws such as the constitution or the ten commandments are followed; however, higher priority is given to principles based on values such as justice, honesty, and equality of human rights.

Mother Teresa lived such principles. She tried to meet not only the physical needs of others, but their soul needs as well. While visiting an orphanage, she was quoted as saying, "There are many in the world dying for a piece of bread, but many more dying for a little love. . . . There's a hunger for love, as there is a hunger for God." Her whole life was dedicated to the value of helping the poorest of God's children.

Characteristics of moral development are universal. We progress through the stages in order. We do not skip stages to progress to a higher stage. If we are on level three, we must go through four to reach stage five.

We may still hold on to prior levels in some areas of decision-making. For example, Mabel may have progressed to level four, following the seventh commandment which states, "Thou shall not steal." But still, she does not consider taking a hotel towel as stealing. This reasoning reflects level two of moral development, "I paid too much for the room; they owe me."

We are not ready to grow into the next level of morality until we are intellectually ready. A sign that might signal readiness is the questioning of a value. Readiness is a factor for all growth.

We become aware of the next stage by becoming attracted to it. When we have decisions to make and our present development does not produce a satisfactory solution, we begin to look elsewhere. Crisis can also create the motivation we need to move or to grow. In crisis we look for alternatives to solve our dilemmas. Crises create change. Change is needed for growth.

Reflection

❧ What stage of morality encompasses most of your decision-making?

❧ Is it the same as where you were ten years ago?

❧ What happened to move you to a new stage?

❧ What values have you derived from this stage?

❧ Are you comfortable here or has God "encircled you and rested his hand on your soul" to grow?

18
Creativity: Strengthening the Soul

Soul strengthening happens as we tend to the issues of everyday living. If we can be creative as we go about the ordinary tasks of life, our soul will find the nourishment it needs to grow. Creativity can emerge or intensify with aging. Legend has it that the swan sings only once in its life, as it approaches death. We need to reframe our thinking if we believe that creativity comes only in youth. Generations have identified age with wisdom, not creativity. We now know that after 50 there is a huge growth spurt in creativity, particularly in women who have been primary caregivers in families. By this time our family and work responsibilities have diminished. We have accumulated all these life experiences and are ready to be redirected into creativity.

As we age we have more time to seek out new or forgotten interests. We are aware of our mortality, and everyday living becomes more valued. We do not want to waste precious time. We are less concerned about what others think about us, and our time is not spent worrying about others' opinions of us. We know where we are and have the freedom of aging to express it. These are factors that encourage creativity.

The world we live in today has opened windows of opportunities for our creative impulse. New approaches to health care help us live more comfortably and extend our lives. The aging of baby boomers provides a powerful lobbying group for seniors. Women are being recognized and acknowledged as late bloomers in their accomplishments. Their creativity is shining like a light for others.

There are countless examples of older women in their 50s, 60s, 70s, and 80s who exhibit their creativity in many ways. They challenge old assumptions and take risks. Women-turned-authors, women going back to school, women volunteering in their areas of interest, or women entering the work force with proof of their life experiences proudly displayed on their resumes provide models for us. They are changing the way we look at aging. They have decreased the fear of it.

At seventy-nine Dorothy was in good health. She and her husband Don had done all the expected retirement activities. They visited their children and grandchildren. They were financially able to travel to distant places at least once a year. They had hobbies of gardening, volunteering, and collecting. They had "been there, done that." But something was missing for them. One day as Dorothy picked up the newspaper from her mailbox, their lives were changed. An ad asked for seniors who would like to go back to work. A well-known department store was hiring older folks as greeters and helpers for their customers. Dorothy and Don were hired, the first married couple to be employed. They loved their work. They were able to work part-time and still have time for the other activities they did before. Best of all, they felt valued.

Let's explore other ways to strengthen our souls:

Strive for a healthy body and alert mind: they are gifts we can bring to our souls. Physical activity that includes exercise, healthy eating habits, and preventative medicine keep our bodies in top condition. This gift of body strength allows our souls to be spiritually healthy. Without major concerns for physical wellness, our souls can aspire to eternal growth.

Keeping the mind alert allows us to touch our souls for intimate communication. Soak up knowledge. It will trickle to the soul and empower spirituality. Read, take a course on a subject you have never explored before, learn a new language, learn to play a musical instrument, join a theater group, or take a cooking class.

Get in touch with your feelings. Keep them from becoming troublesome. Share feelings with a friend. It's OK to cry. It's OK to be wrong sometimes. Try to see the other person's view. If emotions get out of control, see a counselor. Use feelings to reach that deepest part of you, your soul.

Know your limits. Set goals that are challenging, but attainable. Accept change. Tap into your soul for wisdom to change what you are able to change. You'll know you have been successful when you experience the feeling of inner peace.

Make time for humor. Play and have fun. Bring sunshine to your soul. Look for the positive in others and in situations. Approach life with confidence. Affirm your existence.

Be a participant. Become involved with others. When you reach out, you expand your horizons. Your soul will not be confined. It needs freedom to soar.

Get organized. Make lists. Prioritize. Handle the most important issues first. Cross off completed tasks for a sense of accomplishment. Organization creates order. Order creates time for perfecting spirituality.

Learn to relax. Create a quiet scene. Read a book. Listen to quiet music. *Dream.* Let your thoughts carry you to pleasant places. Open yourself to listening to your soul.

Make time to pray. Prayer is the connection to the soul. It is the soul, infused with divine love, that connects us to eternity. Divine love, that love that comes to us from God, comes without any effort on our part if we allow it to touch us. It is as Saint Teresa of Avila described so beautifully, "watering by rain." That's the best and easiest way to care for our inner garden. It is up to us to make use of that divine love by acting in ways that are compassionate and loving, not only for our spiritual development but to connect to others.

We need to pray with confidence, willing to accept God's answer. This answer may not be what we expected, but who knows better than God what is best for us? We must also pray with perseverance. Even though our prayers do not seem to be answered, we need to continue the communication with God. A parent, wise from knowledge and experience, may refuse a child his petition. But if there is a foundation of unconditional love, communication continues. So it is with God.

Prayer gives us spiritual direction. Ask for it. Then listen for an answer. Silence creates the environment for God to communicate with us. Mother Teresa once commented:

> I always begin my prayer in silence. It is in the silence of the heart that God speaks. We need to listen because it's not what we say but what he says to and through us that matters. As blood is to the body, prayer is to the soul.

Reflect on this beautiful song of Saint Bernard. His words describe contemplation, the highest form of prayer:

> It consists not in words of the mouth, but a song of the heart; nor is it a sound with the lips, but a movement of joy. It is the harmony not of voices but of wills.

19
The Ideal Woman

Let's create a vision of the ideal older woman. Someone whose image we can mirror. Unlike the Queen in *Snow White,* she is a woman who is not afraid of aging, "who wants to be all used up" before she dies. This woman will be a composite of many women. She will be a mirror for our souls. She will be the challenge and example of how to "celebrate the older us."

In this final chapter, I offer you the insights of three groups of women who participated in "Celebrate the Older You" retreats. These women have had definite ideas about the woman they want to become. Most have expressed the fear of growing old, not knowing what the future will hold for them. They want to feel comfortable and confident as they age. Their insights will provide a composite of what that ideal woman is like.

One such woman, Marion, fears growing old. She expressed her feelings as we sat in a circle during a retreat. She wanted to become a woman who could accept being alone. The fifteen women there were eager to expand their concept of aging. They discussed loneliness as a concern. By brainstorming, they came up with some specific ideas to reframe aging and loneliness:

Acknowledge the feeling.

Give yourself permission to feel the feeling.

Keep track of when and where the feeling manifests itself.

Reframe loneliness into aloneness, solitude, or quiet time.

Use this time to create self.

Risk new interests.

Try a new hobby.

Investigate helping others or explore working.

Distract yourself.

Go shopping. Get out among people.

Read a book.

Pauline's body was wrinkling before her eyes. She expressed her fear of aging and wanted to stop the aging process. This group discussed beauty. What does it mean? They defined surface beauty and deep inner beauty, how one fades and one keeps blooming. Together they designed goals to lessen fears of growing old by concentrating on inner beauty.

Keep life simple. Live in the here and now.

Notice God's beauty around us.

Redefine what success is about. Set new goals that fit later years of life.

Explore creative aging. Become open to new ideas.

Cultivate inner life.

Become connected spiritually through soul-nurturing.

Keep support systems active.

Another group continued their definitions of the older woman they want to be. We went around the circle. Each person was to mention one characteristic they admired in an older woman. The following was the list created:

An independent and confident woman.

A mentally alert woman.

A woman who is visible, talented, and respected.

A woman who takes intelligent risks.

A woman who loves unconditionally.

A woman who has fine-tuned her value system to fit her age and is true to her values.

A woman who can let go of unimportant things and concentrate on things of value.

A woman fully alive who lets her spirituality shine through.

The group finalized their vision of the ideal older woman with a song that said it all. A woman who will:

Let your light shine for all the world to see:

The brightness of your life within, the peace that set you free.

Let your light shine to fill your nights and days;

all will see the deeds you do and give your Father praise.

—Beatitudes (Damean Music)

PSALM REFLECTION

Read Psalm 139 once again:

Lord, you have probed me, you know me:
you know when I sit and stand;
you understand my thoughts from afar.
My travels and my rest you mark;
with all my ways you are familiar.
Even before a word is on my tongue,
Lord, you know it all.
Behind and before you encircle me
and rest your hand upon me.
Such knowledge is beyond me,
far too lofty for me to reach.
Probe me, God, know my heart;
try me, know my concerns.
See if my way is crooked,
then lead me in the ancient paths.

—Psalm 139:1-6, 23-24

❧ In what ways does God probe you to be the woman you want to be?

❧ Have you set your goals to be reachable or is such knowledge beyond you, far too lofty for you to reach?

❧ What are some "crooked ways" you need to change in your life?

❧ In what ways are you nurturing your soul, developing your inner beauty?

❧ What part does prayer and reflection play in "celebrating the older you"?

Let's celebrate the autumn years of our lives with brilliant color as our roots take firm hold in our souls for our passage into the spring of everlasting life.

I thank you, Lord, with all my heart;
before the gods to you I sing.
I bow toward your holy temple;
I praise your name for your fidelity and love.
For you have exalted over all
your name and your promise.
When I cried out, you answered;
you strengthened my spirit.

—Psalm 138:1-3

Additional copies of *Celebrate the Older You; Becoming a Wiser, Warmer, Mature Woman* and related titles may be purchased at a local religious bookstore or from Ave Maria Press

OF RELATED INTEREST . . .

Midlife Awakenings
Discovering the Gifts Life Has Given Us
Barbara Bartocci
"...offers wisdom, personal experience, and practical help, along with warm assurance that God is there to guide us all through midlife and beyond. Read it, then share it."
—Joan Webster Anderson, author of *Where Angels Walk*   **$9.95***

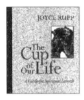

Loving Yourself More
101 Meditations for Women
Virginia Ann Froehle, RSM
Provides a moment of calm amidst the many demands of the day and a gentle reminder of God's constant and sustaining love.
$5.95*

The Cup of Our Life
A Guide for Spiritual Growth
Joyce Rupp, OSM
Shares how the ordinary cups that we use each day can become sacred vessels that connect us with life and draw us even closer to God.   **$11.95***

May I Have This Dance?
Joyce Rupp, OSM
A unique invitation to join with God in the dance of life, an invitation to experience God in the daily and seasonal rhythms of life.   **$10.95***

The Masculine Spirit
Resources for Reflective Living
Max Oliva
Presents men with a clear and resonant call to take up the practice of self-reflection and grow to the fullness of integration and wholeness.   **$8.95***

  To request a complete catalog contact
AVE MARIA PRESS
Notre Dame, Indiana 46556
Phone 1-800-282-1865 ~ Fax 1-800-282-5681

* prices subject to change